# Elco PTs
## IN ACTION

Jack Coggins

# THE STORY OF THE U. S. NAVY'S MOTOR TORPEDO BOATS
## by Electric Boat Company

ISBN #978-1-935700-40-1

# FOREWORD

The effectiveness and versatility of the Navy's potent Elco PTs have been among the sensations of this war.

The toll of enemy ships, planes and men taken by these speedy combat craft—often against heavy odds—is out of all proportion to their small size and relatively low cost.

Elco PTs have sunk or damaged a huge Jap battleship, several cruisers, 15 to 20 destroyers, at least two submarines and many merchant vessels. They have shot down scores of planes and have destroyed hundreds of enemy troop-carrying barges, many of them fully loaded with men and equipment. They have carried commandos on fast hit-and-run raids and covered our landings on Axis-held shores. And they've completed countless daily missions on patrol in enemy-infested waters.

Today Elco PTs are in action in the Mediterranean and the South Pacific, in the English Channel and the Aleutians, in Hawaii and in the Panama Canal area. As the war increases in intensity, more and more swift, deadly Elcos are being rushed to the naval war fronts of the world. New uses, more effective tactics are being discovered and developed for these versatile battle boats. And day by day new exploits are recorded as communiques tell of actions by "light naval craft"—the fabulous PTs.

©2010 Periscope Film LLC
All Rights Reserved
ISBN #978-1-935700-40-1

Elco Naval Division ☆ ELECTRIC BOAT COMPANY ☆ Bayonne, New Jersey

KNIGHTS OF THE SEA

# To a PT

The Navy's new mosquito boats,
 Tricky swerving reckless craft;
  Seventy feet of streaking fury,
   Bow up, streamlined as a porpoise
    Hurtling through a crust of sea.

  Engines roar with repressed power
   Pull like restive four-year-olds,
    Forward force that pulses under
     Superhuman drive and thunder
      On the rattling high speed turns.

Greater than the men who made them;
 Tougher than the wizened seamen;
  Give no mercy—ask no quarter,
   Knifing through the inky water
    In cascades of diamond spray.

  PT—synonym for beauty;
   Ships that catch a sailor's breath;
    Young aristocrats of power,
     Black machines of speedy death.

M.S.B.

# PT BASE AT TULAGI HARBOR

Tulagi, a small island in the Solomons
group, is a short distance from Guadalcanal. Once held by the Japs, it was
wrested from them to become the PT's
base of operations against the
"Tokyo Express"

*From a painting by Dwight Shepler, Lieutenant, USN*
*Kodachrome by Herber Gehr*

The modern American PT carries the heaviest armament of any boat in the Navy for her size; four torpedoes, depth charges, rapid fire guns and, like a trained boxer, she can hit with either hand. This Elco 80' is ingeniously camouflaged. Rosenfeld Photo

# THE DEVELOPMENT OF THE PT

### Thirty Years Ago, the Motor Torpedo Boat Was an Untried Naval Vessel; Today She Is a Successful and Highly Developed Combat Craft

By W. C. SPECHT, *Commander, USN,* and W. S. HUMPHREY, *Lieut (jg), USNR*

WITH THE passing of sail and the advent of the modern machine age came a new and untried weapon — a small, fast, torpedo carrier which was destined to become our speediest and most streamlined naval vessel. In recent years, perhaps no vessel has created more public interest than the motor torpedo boat. However, her history does not begin with the present conflict but rather had its christening in the sixth year of the twentieth century. By the beginning of the first World War, Italy, Germany and England had all taken an active part in small and fast surface torpedo craft development, and today the motor torpedo boat of one type or another forms an important part of nearly every navy.

Italy made the first progress with a successful torpedo carrying motor boat in 1906 — only 37 years ago. This initiated the development of a boat that at least partially fulfilled the desired requirements by the time the first World War started. They were of a ten-ton design and were 52 feet long. By 1916, the Italian boats were from 50 to 69 feet in length, carried from two to four small torpedoes and one or two machine guns. In general, they were capable of a speed of about 33 knots and had little freeboard. To enable them to approach their objective in silence, they were equipped with two electric motors furnished with storage batteries. These motor torpedo anti-submarine boats, MAS as the Italians called them, were used for attacking surface vessels and sub-

marines, for coastal reconnaissance, escorting seaplanes and mine sweeping.

The significance of such vessels in naval operations can be illustrated by the exploits of the Italian MAS against the Austrian Navy. During the first World War, Austria was receiving many of its supplies from overseas; this gave Italy a good opportunity to attack its maritime communications and ports of call. However, there was considerable question as to which type vessel could best be employed for this task. This was where the idea of using the MAS came into being and, in May, 1916, the organization of the first Italian Motor Torpedo Boat program was completed. The first action was in the form of a raid on the night of June 6th, 1916, on the Bay of Durazzo, carried out by two MAS's from a Brindisi base. The boats were supported by destroyers which towed them most of the way. In the bay, they sighted a large steamer, the *Lukrum,* at anchor. One torpedo was fired resulting in the sinking of that vessel. During that night the Austrians did not discover the presence of the MAS and thus they were uncertain as to the method by which the *Lukrum* was destroyed.

It is interesting to note that the Italian MAS's used aircraft reconnaissance to keep them informed of enemy activity. This was the first instance of the coördination of aerial reconnaissance with motor torpedo boats; the possibilities still remain undeveloped. In the upper Adriatic, during

# Elco PTs

November of that year, aerial reconnaissance over Pola and the Canal of Fesana (near the Austrian Fleet Base) showed important surface units anchored in the Fesana Canal, the entrance to which was protected for several days at a time by a series of logs linked together. Aided by a torpedo boat, which was equipped with apparatus to destroy such obstructions, another boat entered the Canal and made two attempts to torpedo an old battleship anchored there. Although both attempts were frustrated by anti-torpedo nets surrounding the battleship, the exit as well as the entrance to the Canal was effected without damage to the MAS.

In 1917, the MAS's were principally used for protection of surface craft from submarines, for mine laying and for reconnaissance in the vicinity of enemy restricted waters. However, it was desired to use them for work of a more offensive nature. So the Italians decided it was advisable to take the initiative and, after much night reconnaissance around Trieste, plans were developed for torpedoing the two battleships *Wien* and *Budapest*. On the night of December 9th, in a thick fog, two MAS's escorted by other light vessels reached the entrance to the Port of Trieste and, after cutting some metal cables, succeeded in forcing an entrance. After careful search, the battleships were revealed and attacked with torpedoes. The *Wien* was hit and went down immediately, and the *Budapest*, anchored nearby, was hit but only slightly damaged. The MAS's were able to escape, in the confusion that followed, by the same route in which they had entered.

The year 1918 was perhaps the most successful for the Italian MAS's, as their raids did much to hamper the life line of Austrian merchant traffic. Their operations on June 8th of that year against the Canal of Otranto were also successful as they further weakened the Austrian Navy. Large units, escorted by torpedo boats, and MAS's operating independently, made up the striking forces. Two MAS's explored the waters between the rock of Gruizza and Selve. After exploring the area, they came out of the Strait at about 2:00 a.m. and headed slowly toward the open sea to join the other units. About 3:00 a.m., a large cloud of smoke was sighted to starboard and, upon investigation, they found two large warships escorted by ten or more destroyers. One MAS maneuvered into position and fired two torpedoes at the first large warship at a range of about 350 yards. The vessel was the *Szent Istvan*, the most recent ship of her type, and she went to the bottom two and a half hours later, despite all efforts to save her. Successful actions continued and, on October 31st, the nets were forced at Pola and a large warship, the *Viribus Unitis*, was sunk. This resulted in complete revolt and loss of discipline in the Austrian Navy.

The Coastal Torpedo Motor Boat (CMB) was the British version of the small, fast torpedo craft and was developed in 1916 as a result of considerable designing work. They were 40 feet long with a speed of about 30 knots, carried two small torpedoes, three machine guns and a crew of three. These boats were mostly Thornycroft design with a single-step hull. By the end of the last war, Britain had constructed a total of 66 CMB's, of which only six were lost.

The CMB's played an important and spectacular part in

*(Continued on page 44)*

4 *The genesis of the motor torpedo boat, from the early CMB to the modern PT. 1, An early British CMB (coastal motor boat) of the planing type. 2, A 55' British CMB of World War I. 3, "Q III" of the Philippine Commonwealth. Of a class built by Thornycroft prior to the present war, these MTB's were 65' in length and carried two 18" torpedoes. 4 & 5, Elco PT's of the latest design. 80' o.a. and carrying torpedoes, depth charges and numerous rapid fire guns. They have won an enviable combat record.*

*Wide World, Real, Rosenfeld and Official U. S. Navy Photos*

# ADVANCE PT BASES

Mother ships, which are often converted yachts, and hidden locations on countless faraway islands and atolls, serve as the operational and maintenance bases of MTB squadrons. The crews of these bases are capable of making every type of repair, even to the extent of major engine installations or rebuilding sections of a hull

Left, the after deck of the mother ship is an improvised officers' mess. Middle right, the "main street" of the PT base at Calvertville, on Florida Island. Over it hangs this sign: "Through these portals pass the best MTB flotilla in the world." Lower right, wash day on a PT in a South Sea hideaway. Acme, International News and Official U. S. Navy Photos

Above, aboard a PT tender, three of her crew prepare to supply one of her brood with a fresh supply of torpedoes. Below, left, the bombed and shell-swept shore line of Tulagi Island as it appeared during the battle for its control. Once occupied by the Japanese, it is now an important U. S. base. Lower left, a makeshift shelter on the forward deck of a PT

Commander Alan R. Montgomery likens the team play of a PT squadron to the well-drilled work of a football team. "The signals are called when we leave the dock, that's all. From there on, the crews depend on their team mates." Acme Newspictures

# SQUADRON "X"

### Theirs Was the Job of Patrolling Between
### Guadalcanal and Tulagi — and They Did It Well

### By HUGH B. CAVE

"YOU GUYS may like the idea of squatting around on cots for the next couple of years," said Chief Torpedoman Hobert Denzil Wisdom, emptying his dungaree pockets of nails which he had pilfered from the carpenter shop, "but me, I got to have comforts." Snorting disdainfully, he sawed a board in half and nailed the pieces into place. Under his capable hands, a sturdy chair was taking shape.

The men grinned. But Wisdom worked on. In front of his tent lay an assortment of lumber and tools, also "borrowed" from the shop. Wiz was busy building furniture. It was good furniture, too.

"The trouble with you guys," he growled, "you're not civilized."

"Maybe," said Gunner's Mate Teddy Kuharski, "you figure to be here forever, huh? Maybe you expect to settle down and raise a family here." With a wink at the others, he placed a hand delicately on his hip and cocked his nose in the air — a dowager at a lawn party. "These, my deah,

are our South Sea cousins, the Tulagi Wisdoms. Ah, yes. So unfortunate."

Wisdom grinned back but his hammer banged away without interruption. He put the chair beside a table he had constructed, then hauled another slab of lumber from the pile and applied try-square and pencil. Something puzzled him. Scratching his chin, he sat in the newly finished chair and for a moment was deep in thought.

Some of the others were building furniture, too; inspired, perhaps, by Wisdom's energy and the undeniable need for a few crude comforts. Comforts were scarce on Tulagi. This particular group of PT men, members of a squadron commanded by then Lieutenant Commander Alan R. Montgomery, of Warrenton, Va., had moved into a section of the torpedo boat base located midway between the huddled shacks on the shore and the lookout post on the bluff. They referred to it as "Snob Hill" and considered it an exclusive suburb.

Radioman George Gilpin came up. He was a dark haired

"The usual attack procedure, once the enemy is sighted, is to close in at high speed, lay down their smoke screen, let go their torpedoes and then duck back into the smoke." OWI Photo

The PT's have speed, drive, swing, change of pace, power and deception. Rosenfeld Photo

southern lad with a sly sense of humor and a grin that could be hidden when necessary behind a studied lack of expression. "I got an idea," he said. "We ought to have some street signs around here to keep you guys from getting lost."

"We ought to have some streets, too," said Chief Torpedoman Elvie O'Daniel, "to get lost on."

"Will you birds shut up?" groused Wisdom. "I'm concentrating."

"He's concentrating," said Gunner's Mate Roy Beckers. "Everybody stand back."

"We need a place to shoot the breeze," Wisdom said. "We need a bench. I'm going to build a bench."

"The Seat of Meditation," said O'Daniel.

"He don't mean that kind of bench," Gilpin argued. "Besides, where would we get any mail order catalogs in this place?"

"I mean a bench to sit on," said Wisdom. "So we can enjoy the view here and shoot the breeze. It gets too damn hot inside these tents and shacks, and there's too many bugs. Leave me alone, you guys. I got to dope out a bench."

He built one. It was finished a couple of days later and occupied a place of honor on "Main Street," where the boys could sit back and look out over the settlement below and the sea beyond On clear days, the sea was a soft, translucent green, very pretty.

The airplane is probably their most dangerous opponent, but they are armed to fight them off and bring them down. Acme Newspictures

It was a different sea at night. Too often, under cover of darkness, Jap destroyers or cruisers came "down the Slot" from Bougainville to put troops ashore on Guadalcanal and to shell exhausted American Marines encamped around Henderson Field. The midget mosquito boats of Squadron "X" patrolled the bloody waters between Guadalcanal and Tulagi, to prevent enemy infiltration. That was their job.

It was grueling work, nerve-racking work, murderous on men and boats alike. For the PT men, those October-November nights of 1942 were long indeed. The fate of Guadalcanal still hung in the balance.

Ashore, the men made the best of what they had. Inspired by Wisdom's work, the occupants of Snob Hill shed their dungarees in the broiling heat of those long afternoons and pitched in to make their surroundings homelike. They swept out the native huts and constructed shelves and cupboards. They put up pictures of wives and sweethearts, built tables for red dog and poker, dug trenches to carry off the rain water which otherwise would have inundated them.

It was terribly hot. Though nearly naked, the men oozed perspiration which attracted swarms of insects. Behind them, Tulagi's gaudy hills rose tawny and green, flecked with flowers and streaked by the passage of brilliant red and snowy white parrots. It was an unhealthy gaudiness, dank and stifling. No one was eager to explore it.

Tables and chairs grew in abundance, and the "snobs" enjoyed unheard of comforts in their high suburb. On the Seat of Meditation, the problems of the war were solved in heated bull sessions. Chief Machinist's Mate Halward Peterson remembered the good times in Panama. Gunner's Mate Leon Nale, a tall, slender lad from Alabama, talked wistfully of the girls he knew. Gilpin and O'Daniel ribbed each other. John Legg taught other quartermasters the finer points of navigation. It was a little like a front porch at home.

"These islands," said one of the men one evening; "these lousy, stinking islands — what good are they? For all of me, the Japs can have 'em. Nobody but a goddam Jap would want 'em!"

(Continued on page 46)

Rosenfeld Photo

# THE PT'S BOX SCORE

PT's Were Credited with Shooting Down
Three Jap Planes at Pearl Harbor, and
They Have Been in Combat Ever Since

*During a recent operation in New Guinea, American PT's served not only as troop transports but also covered landing barges during their attack on Nassau Bay. Here, with a heavy gun mounted on her forward deck, a PT inches in as one of her crew takes soundings. Official U. S. Navy Photos*

ON DECEMBER 7th, 1941, there were two squadrons of Elco PT's in the Pacific, of which one was at Pearl Harbor and the other in the Philippines. When Japan struck her treacherous blow at Pearl Harbor, Squadron One, consisting of twelve boats — half of which were loaded on a fleet oiler — was pressed into immediate action. The boats of Squadron One were, therefore, the first PT's to engage in enemy action and were credited with shooting down three Japanese planes. They were in constant demand for several months after that eventful day for inshore anti-submarine patrol and were the only vessels available which were able to drop depth charges in the shallow, restricted waters of the harbor and channel where enemy midget submarines were lurking, and get clear before the charges exploded. In view of the constant reports of Japanese midget submarine activity in and around Pearl Harbor (many of which were false), and the fact that one or two midget submarines did gain access to the harbor, the presence of the motor torpedo boats and their anti-submarine operations were reassuring to authorities concerned. These PT's possibly accounted for two enemy submarines. This squadron later went from Pearl Harbor to Midway under their own power and there took part in the defense of that island.

The accomplishments of Squadron Three in the Philippines under the command of Lieut. (now Lieut. Comdr.) John D. Bulkeley, USN, which are generally known, have already become an historical part of the first battle of the Philippines. The first major exploit was an attack on a Japanese auxiliary cruiser in Subic Bay. This hard pushed night attack resulted in the cruiser being sunk. The second mem-

orable accomplishment was the sinking of a Japanese 6000-ton auxiliary aircraft carrier. This was a daring raid which made it necessary for the boats to dodge through an inferno of lead from shore batteries and through obstructing nets. One night, while patrolling in the darkness of a tropical storm near Corregidor, an armed landing barge was sighted, attacked and sunk. The barge and 50 troops, apparently bent on landing on Bataan, were destroyed. From this barge two prisoners were taken, a captain and a private, plus their papers and dispatches, which proved of considerable value to American forces. A few days later this squadron scored again by bagging three Japanese dive bombers.

The PT's soon took off on another tour of destruction. This time it was an attack on a 6000-ton Japanese cruiser. The attacking boats were picked up by searchlights, heavy gunfire was directed on them, yet they again came through in fine style by torpedoing the Nipponese vessel. The next day she was found beached, and was later broken up for scrap. The next action was another night raid made by two boats into an enemy occupied harbor on the Philippine coast. The prey was a 10,000-ton enemy tanker moored to the dock. She also was torpedoed and was found still burning the next morning.

Further accomplishment for the Squadron was an act of mercy. When the S.S. *Corregidor*, loaded with 1200 persons, was sunk by a mine in the channels near Corregidor Island, the PT's were the only vessels that came to the rescue. Dodging across the mine fields, they picked up over 105 survivors and carried them safely to Corregidor. There was also the hazardous evacuation of General MacArthur and his party. This proved to be a difficult task for the Squadron,

*An unceasing watch for enemy planes is kept
as the landing craft move in toward the beach*

yet it was a complete success. Proceeding through heavy seas into enemy controlled waters was an accomplishment that will long be remembered. A few weeks later, Manuel Quezon, President of the Commonwealth of the Philippines, was evacuated by a boat attached to Squadron Three. This episode was also packed with narrow escapes from the time the boats left Negros Island until they returned to Mindanao.

Perhaps one of the most important operations of Squadron Three was the torpedoing and sinking of a light cruiser of the *Kuma* class. Receiving word that a Japanese cruiser escorted by destroyers was heading for Cebu, two PT's set out for a night attack on the enemy force. Near midnight, the force was sighted and the enemy was closed to decisive range. One boat, commanded by Bulkeley, drew the fire of the cruiser so that the other, commanded by Lieut. Kelly, could get in her shots. Bulkeley's torpedoes missed but Kelly managed to hit the enemy's magazine and she went down

*A landing barge comes alongside a PT to take on another load*

by the stern in less than 20 minutes. But the fight was not over, as the escorting destroyers gave chase and only good fortune saved the first boat. Kelly was not quite so fortunate, for dive bombers caught up with him next morning in a narrow river where he was unable to maneuver. He shot down one of the attacking planes but the gunfire of the other proved too much for the PT's wooden hull, and Kelly was forced to beach and destroy his boat after many of the crew

*Although the PT's which engaged in these operations came out unscathed, the fortunes of war are such that a certain number of vessels are apt to be lost. This is what a Jap aerial bomb did to one American MTB*

were injured or dead. The remaining six boats of this squadron were finally destroyed by their own personnel to keep them from falling into enemy hands, but this was done after they had taken a tremendous toll of enemy ships and lives.

Japanese night operations in the Solomon Islands created a great demand for PT boats in that theater. Motor torpedo boat Squadron Two, in Panama, consisting of 14 Elco 77-foot boats and augmented by six new Elco 80-footers, was divided into two squadrons — Squadron Two and a new Squadron Three — and these were shipped to the Solomons. Shortly after their arrival at Tulagi Harbor, they participated in their first battle on October 13th, 1942. Squadrons Two and Three were then organized under a Flotilla Commander as MTB Flotilla One, and subsequently participated in 17 actions against Japanese task forces which included destroyers, cruisers and battleships. They were later joined by other PT's which took part in the last engagements.

*Troops board a barge after having been brought in by the PT's*

Prior to the arrival of the PT's, heavy and light Japanese surface ships made almost routine nocturnal excursions from their northern bases, landed troops and supplies on the Japanese-held portion of the island and mercilessly shelled our Marine positions near Henderson Air Field. Except for the hazards created by uncharted coral reefs and the lack of base maintenance and overhaul facilities, the area was ideal for PT boat operations and they proceeded to inflict much damage on enemy vessels. Their activities are considered to have been an important factor in permitting our forces to take over complete control of Guadalcanal, as is indicated by these highlights of some of their engagements:

On October 13th, 1942, Japanese cruisers and destroyers came in to shell Henderson Field under cover of darkness.

*(Continued on page 48)*

An experimental Scott-Paine MTB, the early prototype of the modern Elco PT, arrives from England by steamer in 1939. Wide World Photo

The Navy comes to inspect PTs under construction. R to L; H. R. Sutphen, Admiral R. E. Ingersoll, Rear Admiral O. N. Hustvedt, P. L. Sutphen

The christening of one of Elco's first PTs was a colorful occasion. Mrs. W. N. Bannard, III, and Lt. Comdr. ("We Were Expendable") Bulkeley

Months before Pearl Harbor, the first PT squadron was secretly shipped to the Pacific. Here are six boats loaded aboard a tanker. Elco Photo

Snugged down in an Hawaiian harbor, this squadron of Elco PTs made a name for itself after the Pearl Harbor attack. U. S. Navy Photo

Criss-crossing the stern of an aircraft carrier, a PT here aids the destroyers in screening a large American task force. U. S. Navy Photo

Proudly displaying an insigne showing thirteen enemy craft to their credit are PT skippers Lieuts. Robinson and Searles. USN Photo

The "Niagara" (ex "Hi-Esmaro"), which had served as a PT mother ship, set afire by Japanese planes in the Solomon Islands. USN Photo

Motor torpedo boats even serve as "prison ships." Here one heads for Guadalcanal with a cargo of Tojo's former aviators. Press Assn.

A PT after having been hit by Japanese dive bombers at Rendova Island. Note the crew still busy at the stern guns. Press Assn. Photo

A spectacular role was played by MTBs in the Italian invasion. Here are two alongside an LST in a Sicilian harbor. U. S. Navy Photo.

The first of a new class of AGPs (PT mother ships) hits the water at the Lake Washington Shipyards, Houghton, Wash. U. S. Navy Photo

# THE PT'S AIR ARM

Aerial Reconnaissance for the PT's at Tulagi
was of Great Strategic Value, Even Though
the Price of Gas was Frankly Exorbitant

By GEORGE POLK

*Lieutenant, USNR*

*The author and a native named "Shemuel," who was one of a party which rescued Lieut. Polk when he was shot down during a flight north of Guadalcanal*

OUR PRIMARY mission was flying night reconnaissance for the PT boats. In our pontoon-equipped SOC-type seaplanes, we ranged north and west from our island stronghold as the "eyes aloft" of the PT squadrons guarding the Guadalcanal-Tulagi area. The targets we sought for the motor torpedo boats were the warships of the "Tokio Express," that Jap task force which "rode the Slot" swiftly into the southern Solomons on shelling raids against Henderson Field and American shipping at Tulagi. Frequently, the PT-SOC forces rallied to the radio hunting call: "Enemy sighted!" The Express was running. The hard-hitting torpedo boats and the scouting seaplanes often were all that prevented Jap warships from raking shore positions and merchant ships with point blank gunfire.

The PT boats had been rushed into the fight in the Solomons soon after United States Marines had captured, on Guadalcanal, the Jap-constructed flying field later known as Henderson, and the naval base enclosed by the islands of Tulagi, Florida, Makambo, Tanambogo and Guvutu. After the savage battle for possession of the field and base had ended in American favor, the Japs returned again and again, with ever increasing anger, in attempts to retake his former fortress.

The original motor torpedo boat contingent, hurriedly transported to the South Pacific, arrived in the battle zone with little or no equipment except their boats and a good supply of torpedoes and .50 caliber ammunition (which was found extremely effective for shooting out Jap searchlights). The PT base was set up in Tulagi Harbor and gasoline and tools were borrowed and snitched from any and all unguarded supply dumps. The crews took their craft out at dark, patrolled and attacked all night, returned at dawn. They then refueled with hand pumps from 50-gallon gaso-

line drums, checked the engines, and manhandled new torpedoes aboard. After the chores were done, they tried to get some sleep — while American Marine and Navy pilots from Henderson fought Jap bombers and fighters overhead.

It quickly became apparent that the waters off Guadalcanal and Tulagi were too large to be patrolled adequately by the limited number of motor torpedo boats available. A group of seaplanes, manned by United States Navy pilots and radiomen-gunners, was detailed to assist. The airmen arrived in much the same manner as had the PT crews, equipped with the tools of their trade and little else. Another scramble for gasoline, tents, cots, blankets, mess gear and food ensued and the first United States Naval Air Station in the Solomons was established. (Henderson was a Marine field.)

Since the two groups were to work together, a gentleman's agreement was made that their respective stock piles would be left unmolested. Vitally needed items were scarce, however, and it was agreed that any outsider's provisions were fair game. The two bases shortly became a tribute to American "ingenuity." The two groups functioned as one from their first night of coöperative action. On dark nights, with little or no moon, the "Express" could be counted on to be running. Every boat and plane had part in the plan of attack. It was only during the periods of bright moonlight that the men of the PT base and the air station found a slight break in the routine, for on those lovely nights the Jap was fairly certain to stay at home.

But the tropical moonbeams brought other worries: "Washing Machine Joe," "Maytag Charlie," "Lou the Louse." "Joe-Charlie-Lou" was a light Jap bomber which

SOC's (cruiser scouting planes) such as these teamed up with the PT's to smash the "Red Ball Express" which swept through the "Slot." They made an unbeatable team. Official U. S. Navy Photo

cruised around overhead hour after hour with an engine that went "put-put-put . . . chug-chug . . . put-put-put . . ." He sounded like the small gasoline engines used to drive washing machines; hence his name. (Sometimes he had other names, too. Unprintable names.)

The "washing machine" pilot packed a punch in the form of a 500-pound bomb but was careful never to drop it until he had been overhead for four or five hours. This meant many hours of lost sleep for those below since not until the bomb was safely deposited could anyone rest easily. The mechanics of the two bases maintained stoutly that they were unconcerned about the bomb but that the engine banged and clanked so horribly that no self-respecting grease monkey could sleep through the din. If a plane took off to attack the "Louse," the Jap ducked into a convenient cloud and disappeared. An hour or so later, he would be back, wheezing and clattering away overhead.

Sitting on the edge of foxholes listening to "Lou" was not all lost time, however, for often these hours were the only time available for working out PT-SOC night tactics in theory. During these hours, motor torpedo boat captains and seaplane pilots planned methods of intercepting the "Tokio Express."

We devised tricky passwords to be exchanged between boats and planes so that an English-speaking Jap would not be able to upset and turn off-course an attack. We laughed about the night when the big radio station at Henderson Field had demanded officiously, in the midst of a running fight, the countersign for a certain message. One of the pilots, a busy man at the moment, had shouted into his radio: "God damn it, Henderson, get the hell off the air!" And the Henderson

Field operator, with a sense of humor that made everyone on the radio network chuckle, had answered sweetly: "Thank you, sir. That's good enough."

The captains and pilots argued about the price of gasoline in the Solomons, recalling the time that one of the planes, in the excitement of a prolonged night action, had remained in the air so long that its gasoline had run out. The seaplane had landed in the water near Savo Island, not far from a group of Jap destroyers. The pilot called a PT boat in an embarrassed tone and asked for a few gallons, giving directions as to his location. In a few moments, the boat glided alongside the plane and preparations were made to pass a five-gallon bucket to the radioman-gunner who climbed out on the wing. The two crews waited breathlessly for the transfer. A brief conversation ensued between the man on the wing and the group of men on the stern of the boat. Expecting a Jap searchlight to flick on them at any moment, the PT captain finally demanded in a fierce whisper: "Hey, what's going on back there?"

The PT boatswain growled back: "This *aviator* guy just wants to pay us 17 cents a gallon but we're holding out for 20."

When the bucket had been handed over and its contents spilled into the aircraft tank, the plane was able to taxi away in the darkness. The PT returned to the scrap.

Sitting there in the foxholes, waiting for the "washing machine" bomb to drop, we commiserated one another on the hazards of our respective operations, joking about the dangers of navigation and night take-offs and landings among the unlighted reefs of Tulagi Harbor. The pilots told tall stories of diving at the Jap warships so that their back-seatmen could throw Jap beer bottles at the officers on the bridges. (The beer bottles had been captured — empty — along with other spoils in the Tulagi landing.)

The SOC squadron insignia was designed there in the holes: Disney's character Dopey peering cautiously at something on the dim and darkened horizon. As one pilot remarked: "You've got to be a real 'Dopey' to make more than one flight like these!"

(Continued on page 45)

International News Photos

Above, the gunner of this Elco PT has drawn a bead on an overconfident Jap plane. Five seconds later — "scratch one Tojo." Right, at twilight, two boats start out on the night patrol

# KEY

1 – Melville, R.I.
2 – Miami, Fla.
3 – Canal Zone
4 – Mediterranean
5 – Aleutian Is.
6 – Hawaiian Is.
7 – Midway I.
8 – Philippine Is.
9 – Solomon Is. &
      New Guinea

▲ – Training Centers
● – Areas of Operation

# PTs FIGHT WHEREVER THE ENEMY MAY BE

These maps are graphic proof of the range and variety of PT combat operations. At Melville, R. I. and Miami, Florida, each squadron receives its training; thereafter they are assigned to any one of the many farflung theaters of operation

In the Southwest Pacific, PTs put the "Tokyo Express" and the "Bougainville Barge Line" out of business; now they are gaining new laurels in New Guinea. In the Mediterranean, they are participating in amphibious operations of every kind

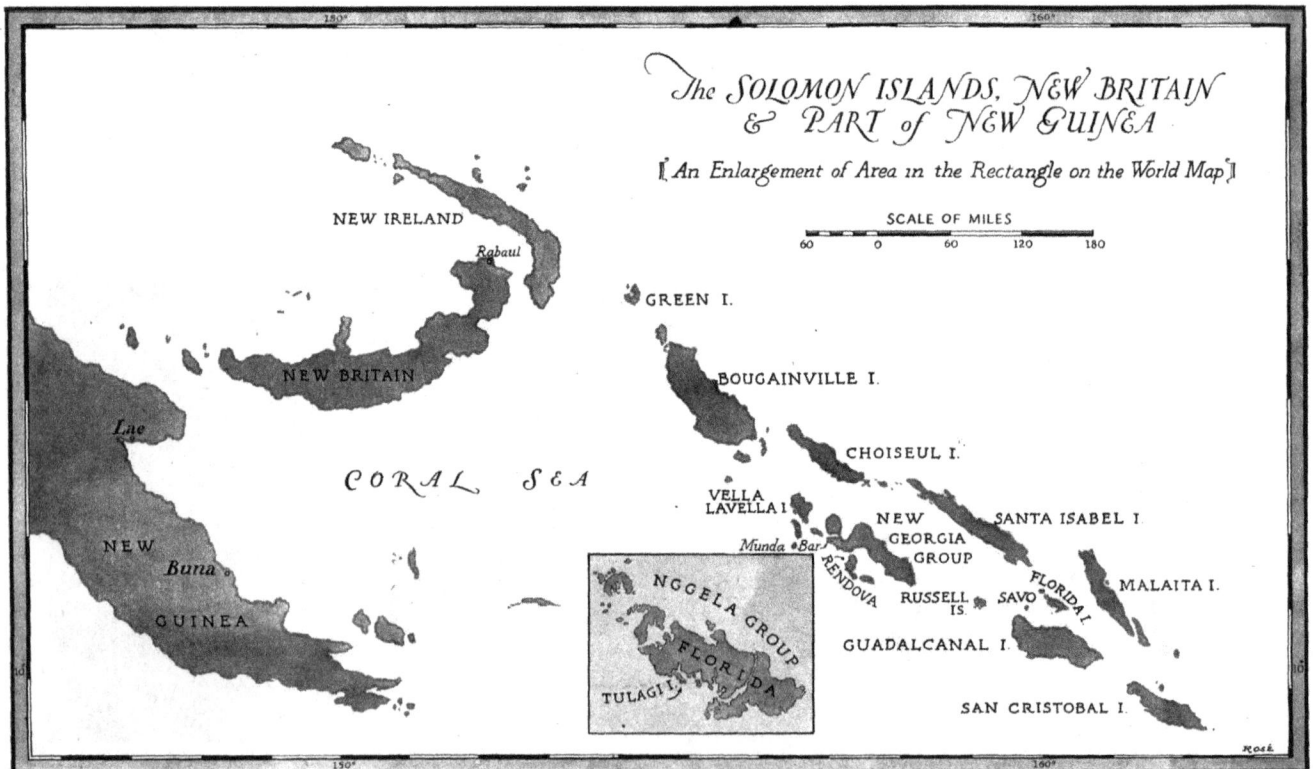

The SOLOMON ISLANDS, NEW BRITAIN & PART of NEW GUINEA

[An Enlargement of Area in the Rectangle on the World Map]

SCALE OF MILES

*To the west of Alaska stretches the long chain of islands which form the Aleutian Archipelago. Bleak and forbidding, many of them are nothing more than volcanoes. PT patrols in these boisterous waters were no picnic. Press Association Photo*

# NORTH OF LATITUDE 49°

### PT Operation in the Aleutian Chain is a Punishing Assignment
### For There the Wind Blows 90 m.p.h. and Even the "Head" Freezes

IT WAS late in the summer of 1942 when our Division of Elco PT's was outfitted in Seattle in preparation for duty in Alaskan-Aleutian waters. Since none of the officers and men had had experience in the North Pacific, we were dependent upon the local officers and civilians for advice in choosing both clothing and gear. Each member of the crew, prior to our departure, was furnished with a muskrat fur hat, lumber jacket, woolen shirts, and "tin" pants in addition to the equipment normally furnished all naval vessels. We were even advised to carry special mosquito nets for protection against the "no-see-'um," which are tiny mosquitoes capable of flying through the usual netting without so much as folding their wings!

When the boats were fully ready, we departed in company for the Aleutians *via* the Inside Passage. The first difficulty was encountered at night off the mouth of the Fraser River when the division leader mistook the lights of fishing vessels for navigational lights on the beach and ploughed through, at 25 knots, the nets of some irate fishermen. One boat, commanded by Lieut. Larry Jones, immediately reported a marked propeller vibration and thumping noise but managed to maintain speed until the first refueling port was reached. Crew members, clad only in long handle underwear and shallow water diving helmets, spent many hours in the frigid waters attempting to remove fathoms of line and cork net floats from the propellers and shafts of all boats. No wonder the fisherman had cussed us so emphatically when our torpedo boats roared through.

As we progressed north, all hands were awed by the beauty and majesty of the mountainous terrain bordering the Inside Passage. No one will ever forget the snow-capped peaks, blue glaciers and shores lined with evergreens, reflected on the smooth clear water disturbed only by the brilliant white wakes of our boats. The great abundance of wild fowl, deer, bears and fish thrilled those of us who enjoy the outdoors.

Everyone has heard of the so-called southern hospitality, but the Southland has nothing on the inhabitants of our Alaskan cities. Our personnel were welcomed and enter- tained at every stop, whether city, fish cannery or native village. The Inside Passage to Alaska provides for the yacht enthusiast in peacetime a voyage filled with all the beauties and wonders of Norway. The smooth waters gave us a false sense of security which led us to believe that the tales of high winds and rough seas in the North Pacific were only myths. However, the passage around Cape St. Elias resulted in many seasick officers and men who, as they leaned over the torpedo tubes feeding the fish, wished that they had never heard of the Gulf of Alaska.

Upon arrival in Kodiak, the Division was ordered to proceed out along the Aleutian Chain to an advance base. Good fortune had favored us all the way from Seattle until one of the officers, only a few months gone from the cornfields of Iowa, failing to realize the significance of the red paint on a channel buoy, left it on the port hand when it should have been passed to starboard. Unfortunately, a rock contested his boat's passage — with the boat coming out second best.

This grounding was only the beginning of our maintenance difficulties which became more serious as the weather changed for the worse and our days on patrol increased. Lieut. Matteson, Lieut. Ewell and Machinist Frank Coleman demonstrated great initiative and ingenuity in super-

*Neither temperature nor sea conditions hinder a PT from laying down a highly effective smoke screen. Elco Photo*

15

*During many patrols the Aleutian PT squadron weathered seas which were as rough and choppy as can be found anywhere, yet both the boats and their crews came through with an excellent record. Official U. S. Navy Photo*

vising baling wire repairs to keep the boats operating. No repair crews were available so we were dependent upon the men actually assigned to the boats to keep them in repair as well as to man the armament. Machinist's Mates Hubbard, Tinckham and Brown, Chief Torpedoman Galentine, Chief Radiomen Landrum, Mott, Pierson and Ward spearheaded the repair gang. All hands, no matter what rating, pitched in to keep the boats in condition. For repair jobs beyond the capacity of our limited ship's force the division was compelled to depend upon the Sea Bees, shore bases and Auxiliary vessels.

It was during a major overhaul of the boats on a marine railway in a fish cannery that we all learned to know and love old Barney Sims. Barney was a Cape Codder who had settled down in Alaska in 1901 and had existed ever since by beachcombing, trap-tending and making "sourdough." His quarters consisted of a lean-to shack on the end of a lonely sand spit. Two dogs and an entire family of cats had free run of the house, Barney's bunk, and his other meager furniture. Since Barney was too old to worry about making time with the ladies and didn't care what the men thought, he never shaved or took a bath. But as time went on, he was invaluable in helping with marlinespike seamanship, and his ready wit was a constant source of entertainment.

Berthing and messing was a problem since we were compelled to eat and sleep on board. Our cooks did a noble job of preparing chow on either hot plates or kerosene burners. Their cooking reputation spread and we often had Army personnel dropping in for potluck dinners. The men on the larger vessels felt sorry for us and would often send over pies, fresh meats and fruits. As a result, we bummed the best food from each of them without the others knowing it, and we ate like kings. No one has yet been able to figure out

how the cooks, using only hot plates, roasted those Thanksgiving turkeys intact.

As the winter progressed, the average temperature dropped steadily. During one severe storm, which was accompanied by williwaws which reached wind velocity of over 90 knots, all the plumbing to the heads froze solid. To use this essential gear, it became necessary to thaw it by heating with nothing less than a blowtorch! This was a tedious and dangerous

*One severe storm was accompanied by williwaws which reached a wind velocity of over 90 knots. OWI Photo*

operation and we tried to regulate the crew's living habits so that one daily thawing would take care of the entire outfit.

But, in spite of endless personnel hardships, crowded living conditions and a continual battle with the elements, the personnel held up splendidly. Many of them even gained as much as 20 to 25 pounds during their stay in northern waters. During our many patrols, the boats weathered seas which were as rough and choppy as can be found anywhere. All in all, they stood up well and proved themselves seaworthy and rugged under all conditions.

Looking back, the Division's stay in the Alaskan-Aleutian Area was certainly an eventful one, but there was one unfortunate phase of it: the Japanese never had the courage to come within striking range of us!

*A Navy Catalina (PBY) flying boat glides to a landing at an advanced PT base. In the background, the Aleutian headlands wear a mantle of white fog. Official U. S. Navy Photo*

# PT'S IN THE PACIFIC

Eleven Angry PT's Were Hardly a Match for the "Tokyo Express" Consisting of a Sizeable Jap Fleet, But It Never Got Through

By A. H. HARRIS

*Lieutenant, USNR*

Steel helmets and kapok life jackets are worn by all members of the crew when a PT goes into combat. Here are the skipper, quartermaster and radio man at their stations on the "bridge." Life Photo

THEY GAVE the young lieutenant a tremendous welcome. The town was out in force, the high school band played "Anchors Aweigh," the crowd hemmed him in and the cheering became hoarse. They wined him and dined him, and the speeches were long and laudatory. He was the glamour boy of the PT's, the shining Knight of the Navy, and one of the bravest men who ever had sailed the briny deep. Young boys looked upon him and their souls were stirred with high resolve. Old men envied him and were proud of his achievements. Standing before them, the Navy Cross leading an array of ribbons, he was to his neighbors a fortunate young man indeed; one who had had an opportunity to serve his country in battle and had acquitted himself and thus, vicariously, his neighbors, in the highest traditions of a fighting Yankee Navy. When he went to bed that night, his name was on the lips of everyone. The lieutenant was an authentic hero.

He also was a very tired young man who had lost 30 pounds in weight, whose bloodstream was crawling with malaria, and whose mind was eerie bright with memories of six months of vicious fighting, of fever-ridden jungles, of monotonous food, of exhausting night patrols, of a sweat-soaked existence, and of death that came to friends from enemy shells and hungry sharks. Nobody had talked much about that at the banquet. He wondered if they even had thought about what really made up the life of a PT man.

Like that night, for example, when a Jap shell crashed into the starboard side of his PT, exploded the fuel tank, and threw shrapnel and flames all over the boat. Like the night they intercepted the "Tokyo Express" with 19 destroyers and cruisers in its train. Eleven angry PT's, with an ample supply of highly effective stingers aboard, were ordered to assist in the wreck of that "Express." They did.

The men and officers in PT "X," which was leading a two-boat formation, were as jittery as they were determined. In spite of the fact that they knew Jap planes were hidden in the black night aloft, their stomachs still went tight when a plane spotted them and noiselessly glided down from astern and dropped a large bomb close aboard their beam. The bomb had no effect other than to add much to their already jumpy nerves. The plane went after more important game and the two PT's lay to off the island, their silhouettes fading into the tropical background. The "Express" was due any minute.

PT "X" fired her four torpedoes at close range and turned her stern to head for the base. Her mission was accomplished. But, before she could put safe distance between herself and the enemy, a destroyer caught her in the gun sights, and all hell broke loose; shells began exploding astern and on all sides close aboard. Finally, a shell hit the fuel tanks and exploded, throwing shrapnel and flames all over the boat. This is the way the lieutenant described the next few hours:

"It was every man for himself then, and some of the men must have been blown overboard as the blast was terrific. I scrambled over the sides of the cockpit, by then red with flames, and plunged head first into the water. The boat still was under way, running in a big circle, burning from stem to stern and a flaming target for the Jap shells trying to sink her. Our own ammunition began exploding and made a piker out of Luna Park on the Fourth.

"I was OK and began calling to the others. I found

Right, certain motor torpedo boat squadrons had shark's eyes and mouths painted on their bows. Below, "We seldom know what happens," reported one officer in describing combat tactics. "We may see a flash, but it is not always from the ship that has gone down." International News Photo

A "motor mac," holding his diving gear, completes the servicing of a PT's underbody. Life Photo

Even the bearded "motor mac" down in the engine room wears a life jacket and steel helmet. Life Photo

A PT torpedo man at his station. Note the mallet in his hand. Life Photo

'Sparks.' He was horribly mangled and bleeding badly. The ship's cook joined me and we made a tourniquet for 'Sparks,' using a .45 and pieces of a life jacket to do it. Not so easy, floating around at night in the water with a roaring side show going on close aboard. We started towing 'Sparks' to the island. It seemed the nearest land. And then we heard the Skipper yelling that he was burned so badly that he couldn't remove his helmet or his binoculars. We were busy with 'Sparks,' but a couple of the other fellows went to the Skipper and towed him all night, while fighting sharks. They saved his life that night.

"'Sparks' was in a bad way and that bleeding leg didn't help him or us. The fireman joined our group and lent a hand. Once he said a dead body bumped against him. The dead body was a hungry shark, attracted by 'Spark's' blood. There were a lot of other sharks, too. We thrashed around, fired .45's at any fin we could see or under the water to scare them away. But there were too many and we thought we were done for. When dawn came, planes spotted us and we were picked up by a boat. But not 'Sparks.' The sharks got him."

The advanced base to which the lieutenant returned was a place of great beauty and would have warmed the heart of any Hollywood producer. Tall palms lined the banks. Thatch-roofed villages spawned natives who fished in the lagoon from outrigger canoes. The water was calm and blue and shimmering. The sun rose and set in a riot of color which would have exhausted the vocabulary of a painter-poet. The foliage of the jungle backdrop was rich, and gay birds made their nests amidst the rare flowers. The base also was uncomfortable and treacherous. The calm blue shimmering water hid uncharted reefs that ripped the thin-bottomed PT's to shreds. The thatch-roofed native huts seemed to quiver in a burning heat and flies and mosquitoes and scorpions and spiders were neighbors of the gaily colored birds.

Considering where the base was located and the difficulties of supply, the chow wasn't so bad. But corned willie and pressed ham and many dehydrated vegetables for two weeks straight became a trifle monotonous. And so did canned tuna fish and chicken soup for the next several days, or just native rice and beans. But no one went hungry, and their thirst could be slaked by water hauled from shore springs to the boats by dinghy, life raft and outrigger. Such water sometimes was a bit flat, but refrigeration on the boats and a great plenty of canned fruit juices, pineapples and coconuts and limes (in season) varied the liquid monotony. Occasionally a passing ship or newcomer to the ranks dropped off some beer or brought a precious fifth of something more potent. When that happened, there was a joyous, if brief, celebration.

When he was off duty, and not wrapped in fatigued sleep, the lieutenant was hard put to keep amused. Recreation was scarce and all of them found it a mistake to be idle. Hence their absorption in blackjack, bridge, poker, craps, magazines, aged newspapers and books. Hence their willingness to endure a hoary movie, shown in a hot stuffy messhall jammed with unwashed humanity. Hence their bull sessions, when "shooting the breeze" whiled away the time in nostalgic and relatively harmless thoughts of home comforts in store for those who would return.

Pets were rampant on the base. There was George, a parrot of Aussie lineage, who was an accomplished chow dive-bomber. He rarely lacked for food, even if his master found him a poor conversationalist. The lieutenant's mascot was a squirrel named, naturally enough, "PT." "PT" had a passion for tearing up gun covers, but he always seemed to

(Continued on page 43)

Based on information available as of March 15, 1944

| | | |
|---|---|---|
| AKERS, *Ensign Anthony B.* | [5, 6] | GLOVER, *De Witt L.* [7] |
| AMATHEIS, *Harold L.* | [8] | GOODMAN, *David* [7] |
| ASHMAN, *Lt. Harold D.* | [12] | GREENE, *Lt. (jg) James Brent* [5] |
| ATKINS, *Cdr. Barry K.* | [5] | GRIFFIN, *Ensign William F.* [5] |

AKERS, *Ensign Anthony B.* [5, 6]
AMATHEIS, *Harold L.* [8]
ASHMAN, *Lt. Harold D.* [12]
ATKINS, *Cdr. Barry K.* [5]

BAGBY, *Lee A.* [5]
BAILEY, *Grant R.* [5]
BALOG, *John X.* [7]
BANNARD, *Lt. (jg) William N.* [5]
BARNES, *Lt. Cdr. Stanley M.* [2, 11]
BARTLETT, *George F.* [6]
BAYLIS, *Lt. John S., Jr.* [6]
BECKNER, *Charles C.* [6]
BENNETT, *Harry R.* [8]
BERGIN, *Lt. (jg) Edward R., Jr.* [5]
BERNDTSON, *Lt. Arthur H.* [5]
BURNIE, *Edward L.* [5, 13]
BOUDOLF, *Joseph L.* [6]
BRANTINGHAM, *Lt. Henry J.* [5, 6]
BULKELEY, *Lt. Cdr. John D.* [1, 2, 6, 9*, 10, 12]
BURK, *Lt. Joseph W.* [2]
BURNETT, *Robert B.* [6]

CABOT, *Lt. (jg) Oliver H. P.* [5]
CALVERT, *Capt. Allen P.* [4]
CAMPBELL, *Lt. Cdr. C. M.* [2]
CAREY, *Lt. John L.* [5]
CHALKER, *Joseph C.* [6]
CLARK, *Jesse N.* [6]
CLIFT, *John W., Jr.* [6]
COBB, *Ned M.* [6]
CONN, *LeRoy G.* [6]
CONNOLLY, *Lt. (jg) B. J. III* [2]
COX, *Lt. (jg) George E., Jr.* [2, 6, 9, 10]
CRAIG, *Clayton A.* [5]
CROUCH, *Harold C.* [5]

DANKEY, *Leo J.* [12]
DEAN, *Lt. (jg) Frank H., Jr.* [5]
DE VRIES, *Marvin H.* [6]
DONOHUE, *Ensign Carrol J.* [8]
DU PREE, *Benjamin E., Jr.* [13]

EBERSBERGER, *George W., Jr.* [5]
EICHELBERGER, *Paul E.* [6]
ELLICOTT, *Lt. (jg) Joseph R.* [5]
ELSASS, *Merle C.* [8]
EMMONS, *Lt. (jg) James W.* [5]

FARLEY, *Lt. Edward I.* [5]
FARROW, *Cdr. Henry* [5]
FAULKNER, *Lt. Clark W.* [2]
FOLEY, *Harold William* [8]
FREELAND, *Lt. Frank* [5]

GAISER, *Clinton E.* [5]
GAMBLE, *Lt. Lester H.* [2, 5]
GIACCANI, *Floyd R.*

GLOVER, *De Witt L.* [7]
GOODMAN, *David* [7]
GREENE, *Lt. (jg) James Brent* [5]
GRIFFIN, *Ensign William F.* [5]
GRIZZARD, *Herbert W.* [6]
GUYOT, *Dale* [6]

HABIG, *Ensign Leonard P.* [8]
HAMACHEK, *Lt. Russell E.* [5]
HAMILTON, *Ensign Richard A.* [5]
HAMILTON, *Lt. Stuart* [12]
HANCOCK, *Morris W.* [7]
HARRIS, *David W.* [7]
HOULIHAN, *John L., Jr.* [6, 10]
HUNTER, *Velt L.* [7]

JOHNSON, *Ensign Gene H.* [6]
JOHNSON, *Harold C.* [5]
JOHNSON, *W. H.* [6]

KEATH, *Harry G.* [6]
KELLY, *Lt. Cdr. Robert B.* [2, 6, 9, 14]
KENNEDY, *Lt. John F.* [12]
KONKO, *William F.* [6]
KOZYRA, *Walter A.* [5]
KREINER, *Lt. William E.* [12]

LANGSTON, *Clem L.* [6]
LAWLESS, *John* [7]
LEE, *Wilfred J.* [5]
LEGG, *John D.* [5]
LEIBENOW, *Lt. (jg) William F.* [6]
LEWIS, *John H.* [6]
LICODO, *Benjamin* [7]
LIGHT, *James D.* [7, 10]
LISCHIN, *Richard H.* [5]
LOGGINS, *Lamar H.* [5, 8]
LONG, *Walter L.* [8]
LUCISONO, *Ralph* [5]
LYNCH, *Lt. Robert F., Jr.* [5]

MACAULEY, *Lt. Edward, III* [5]
MAHAN, *Lt. Richard D.* [8]
MARTINO, *John* [7]
MacMILLAN, *Thomas S.* [5, 6]
McADOO, *Lt. Francis H., Jr.* [5]
McELROY, *Lt. (jg) John Edwin* [5]
McEVOY, *James A., Jr.* [6]
MEDYNSKI, *Kornello* [8]
MILLER, *Lt. James E.* [5]
MONTGOMERY, *Lt. Cdr. Alan R.* [5]
MORROW, *Leroy C.* [8]
MURRAY, *Ensign Bond* [6]

NAPOLILLO, *Francis J., Jr.* [6]
NEFF, *Charles E.* [13]
NEHER, *Delbert G.* [5]

NIKOLORIC, *Lt. (jg) Leonard A.* [5]
NOEL, *Otis F.* [6]

OFFRET, *Elwood H.* [6]
OLSEN, *Richard A.* [8]
O'NEILL, *Richard J.* [5]
OSBORNE, *Cletus E.* [5]
OWEN, *Paul A.* [6]

PARRISH, *Benjamin F.* [5]
PAUL, *William E.* [12]
PELLINAT, *Charles A.* [5]
PESSOLANO, *Lt. Michael R.* [5]
PIERSON, *Ernest E.* [6]
POSEY, *William H.* [5]
POST, *Horace C.* [5]

RAY, *Capt. H. J.* [4, 6]
REGAN, *Richard A.* [6]
REYNOLDS, *Willard J.* [5]
RICHARDS, *Lt. (jg) Ralph L.* [5]
RICHARDSON, *Carl C.* [7]
RICHARDSON, *Ensign Iliff D.* [7]
ROBINSON, *Lt. Hugh M.* [5]
ROCKWELL, *Rear Adm. Francis W.* [3, 6]
ROGERS, *Harold E.* [5]
ROGERS, *Patrick M.* [5]
ROME, *Lt. Russel W.* [8]
ROOKE, *Henry C.* [6]
ROSS, *Albert P.* [7]
ROSS, *Ensign George H. R.* [8]
RUFF, *Lt. (jg) John William* [5]

SCHNEIDER, *Lt. (jg) Robert E.* [5]
SEARLES, *Lt. John M.* [2, 5]
SEARLES, *Lt. Robert L.* [5]
SEWELL, *Allen R.* [5]
SHAMBORA, *John* [6]
SHEPARD, *George W., Jr.* [7]
SIMS, *Watson S.* [6]
SNOWBALL, *Lt. Alfred A.* [5]
SPECHT, *Cdr. William C.* [13**]
STAYONOVICH, *Emil P.* [5]
STROUD, *Densil C.* [6]

TAYLOR, *Lt. Henry S.* [5]
TAYLOR, *Lt. Cdr. Leroy* [5]
TRIPP, *Harry P.* [7]
TUGGLE, *John L.* [7]

WALBRIDGE, *Lt. (jg) George O.* [5]
WARFIELD, *Cdr. Thomas G.* [5]
WILCOX, *Walter F.* [5]
WILLEVER, *Stewart, Jr.* [7]
WINGET, *George W.* [6]

YANDO, *Stephen* [5]

N.B. All the men in Squadron "X", as listed in "Long Were The Nights" (Hugh B. Cave's saga of PT Squadron X in the Solomons) have now received the Presidential Unit Citation to the First Marine Division

LEGEND: [1] *Medal of Honor* [2] *Navy Cross* [3] *Distinguished Service Medal* [4] *Distinguished Service Medal — Army* [5] *Silver Star — Navy* [6] *Silver Star — Army* [7] *Silver Star — Army, with Oak-Leaf Cluster* [8] *Navy and Marine Corps Medal* [9] *Distinguished Service Cross — Army* [10] *Distinguished Conduct Star — Philippine* [11] *British Distinguished Service Cross* [12] *Purple Heart* [13] *Legion of Merit* [14] *Gold Star in lieu of a second Silver Star* [*] *with Oak-Leaf Cluster* [**] *for outstanding contributions to the development of PT boats and the MTB training program.*

M. Rosenfeld Photo

"THE FLYWEIGHT SHIP WITH THE HEAVYWEIGHT PUNCH," PT "117," AN ELCO 80-FOOTER

# THE STORY BEHIND "THE EXPENDABLES"

### From the Idea that a Small, Seaworthy Motor Boat Capable of High Speed Would Make a Fighting Ship Has Come a New Type of Sea Warfare

#### By IRWIN CHASE

IT HAS been said that the present war has afforded the small boat the first real opportunity of playing a major rôle as an offensive vessel. Such a statement is undoubtedly open to considerable interpretation, for the ML's, CMB's, sub-chasers and other small boats of World War I wrote a spectacular and unforgettable chapter in the history of that titanic struggle. Yet a frank analysis of today's naval communiqués definitely establishes that the motor torpedo boat is now employed solely as an out-and-out fighter, and her combat record shows that she has sent more enemy ships to the bottom (to say nothing of landing barges and aircraft) than her most ardent advocates ever believed possible. The result is that, from any naval standards, the PT is no longer an untried and semi-experimental craft but is an accepted "weapon of opportunity" which has far from exhausted both her design and combat possibilities.

Although my early training as a naval architect at the University of Michigan was in large ships, my first and only love has always been small vessels. I started working with them at Elco in 1906 and have continued ever since and, during all these years, I was fostering a firm belief that a relatively small motor boat which was seaworthy and capable of high speed would some day write a new chapter in the history of sea warfare. At Elco, our first activity in this direction was early in the last war when we designed and built over 700 80-foot ML's for the British, French and Italian governments in what was then record breaking time. During the winters of 1915-'16 and '16-'17, I went to England to see the boats in actual service and to make suggestions regarding their maintenance and the training of their crews.

It is an undisputed fact that the "father" of the modern American motor torpedo boat is H. R. Sutphen, of the Electric Boat Company, who first visualized their possibilities of use in World War II. In 1938, various developments took place which indicated the possibility of interesting our navy in the employment of a new type of MTB, and in January 1939, armed with the proper introductions, Mr. Sutphen took me to England to get first hand information on the Royal Navy's progress in the development of MTB's. As a result, I was given a most unusual opportunity to see the various types under construction and compare their performances by actual trials. The three designs which interested us most were the Thornycroft, which was a development of the famous CMB's; the Vospers, which had been developed in co-operation with the Admiralty; and Scott-Paine's newest 70-footer. All three showed great advances in speed and seaworthiness over

*The author engaged in a bit of mental arithmetic during a PT trial trip. Rosenfeld Photo*

*Completing the deck framing on one of the early types of Elco PTs. Life Photo by Gabriel Benzur*

anything in the United States and each had its individual points to recommend it. Rough water trials showed that the Scott-Paine model had exceptional seaworthiness and this feature, with a number of other superior characteristics, made us sure that it could best be adapted to the needs of our Navy. Mr. Sutphen placed an order for one of these boats and she was delivered in New York in September, 1939.

I have often been asked what was the underlying cause of Elco's gambling on the motor torpedo boat as a weapon of this war. In retrospect, I suppose the principal reason was because we had had long experience with one basic factor in hull design with which the average naval officer was not familiar: namely, that a small, high speed motor boat could be designed so that she would be fit to go to sea and stay there in any weather. We had learned much with the ML's, weathering winter gales in the North Sea, and still more during the prohibition era from a class of fast weight-carrying boats which alternately served the rum runners and the Coast Guard. The latter notorious craft also proved that a converted aviation engine, properly installed and run within its capabilities, could accomplish propulsion miracles. Few commercial installations of high powered, light weight engines have been given a real chance to show what they could do, not because of the construction of the engine but more often because of faulty conversion and shoddy installation.

The story of the employment of the Packard engine in the American-built PT is a chapter in itself. Colonel J. G. Vincent, the designer of Packard's famous Liberty motor, after seeing our Scott-Paine boat perform with her Rolls Royce engines, became a most enthusiastic MTB supporter and was sure that we could produce an All-American boat which would be even better than was the British. At the outset, we at Elco outlined the performance characteristics which were desired and left it to Packard to develop and perfect an engine that would fulfill these requirements. The result was a success in every respect, not only from a performance point of view but in terms of manufacturing and production considerations as well. It is my sincere belief that the development of this reliable engine was as important a step

*An 80-footer backs out of the derrick-controlled launching cradle following the christening ceremonies. Rosenfeld Photo*

in the evolution of the PT as were the subsequent modifications of the original Scott-Paine boat.

In our development of the PT, the essential features which we have been able to improve were speed, handiness, cruising radius, seaworthiness, structural design and the ability to carry a large "pay load." The "pay load" for a motor torpedo boat is the ordnance consisting of torpedoes, tubes, guns, mounts and ammunition; armor and other things which the enemy might like to know about; crew with their gear; communications — (radio, etc.); and fuel — tons and tons of it. To carry this "pay load" successfully is the real reason for the boats' existence and every pound which can be saved in the design of the hull and machinery means one more pound of effectiveness. Of equal importance, from the Elco point of view, was the necessity of improving the design in terms of modern production methods. All of this meant redesigning the original boat so as to incorporate the employment of the most up-to-date American construction methods, light weight materials, and building a plant which was specifically designed for the job and was equipped with the most advanced types of tools.

These production methods, with resulting interchangeability of parts, proved their worth recently when we were asked to assemble a number of the boats on the West Coast. The Harbor Boat Building Co., of Terminal Island, Los Angeles Harbor, assembled the sets of fabricated parts complete even to the last coat of paint which we shipped them from Bayonne. Inspection and trials held after their completion in record time proved them to be exact duplicates of their Bayonne sisters.

All of these elements of the Elco PT design are important but, to my mind, speed and seaworthiness are the prime essentials. The factors governing speed are pretty well understood (although our trials and experiments are teaching us things every day which are not "in the book") but the question of seaworthiness and how to improve it has puzzled men ever since there was a boat. The specifications which have been written in the past saying, for instance, that "the boat shall be able to make 40 knots in a four-foot sea" were really meaningless because important things such as length of seas between crests, wind force and relative courses were always omitted. It is not the high, long seas which limit the speed of these boats, but it is going to windward through the short steep chop of shoal tidal waters which tests both the boat and its crew. We have run PT trials in seas over 20 feet high at full speed for hours at a time, with no damage to the hull and not a drop of water on deck; on the other hand, at 30-knots in a chop not more than 4 feet high, some of the early hulls were damaged and members of the crews seriously injured.

We are sure that the Elco PT as built today represents a great advance in providing speed with seaworthiness in

*(Continued on page 45)*

*The modern American PT, such as these Elco 80-footers, is as different from her prototype of World War I as the modern bomber is from the warplane of 25 years ago. They range in length from 70 to 80 feet and have a below deck space which houses three powerful Packard motors, an all-electric galley, bunks, radio equipment, ammunition, tools, locker space and a variety of miscellaneous gear for nine men and two officers. Rosenfeld Photos*

# THE PT'S "TEETH"

*The motor torpedo boat is a seagoing "Indian fighter." She seeks out her prey by night, and both stealth and high speed enable her to engage and disengage her foe. Although her adversary may be many times her size and displacement, she is always the first to attack*

*They are fitted with a wide variety of armament especially suited to PT combat. High-angle, rapid-fire guns are not only offensive weapons against planes and ships, but can quickly knock out enemy searchlights. Torpedoes and depth charges pack the punch that enables them to accomplish the objective of every mission: "intercept and destroy"*

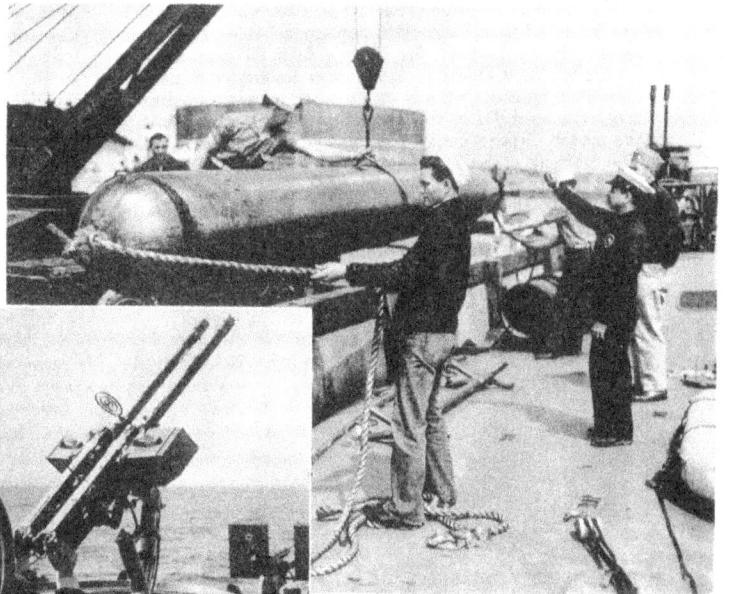

*Vital Statistics of an Elco PT's "Teeth": Forward turret, 20 mm. or 50 cal.; After turret, 20 mm.; Stern gun, 50 cal.; four 21" torpedo tubes; depth charges in quantity. Rosenfeld, OWI, Elco and U. S. Navy Official Photos*

# PT—"PLENTY TOUGH"

## The Motor Torpedo Boat Cut Her Teeth in World War I, Has Won Her Spurs in World War II and Presents Great Possibilities for the Future

### By WALTER ROWE, JR.

*Lieutenant Commander, USNR*

IN THE Navy Department at Washington, just outside the Secretary's office, is a model of the old battleship *Maine,* and if you look at it closely you will see on the boat deck two steam launches of the type peculiar to that period. Upon close examination of these launches, you will discover torpedo tubes mounted in each bow and, until disputed, these little boats should prove to be the first power torpedo boats of the U. S. Navy. They were 61 feet long and typical of the steam reciprocating engine picket boats of that period. The ill-fated *Maine* and her steam torpedo launches were destroyed in Havana Harbor on February 15th, 1898, and it remains for the historians to fill in the blanks from that time until the beginning of 1939, when the President of the United States initiated an active program for the design and construction of motor torpedo boats for our Navy.

The story of Bulkeley's famous "Expendables" and their heroic campaign in the Philippines is now history. That he was able to continue action as long as he did without base repair or maintenance is one of the many miracles of the first months of the war in the Pacific. The PT's at Pearl Harbor, Midway and the Philippines represented the first modification by Elco of the original Scott-Paine 70-foot model which was imported from England in September, 1939, and duplicates built to become our Navy's first PT squadron in December, 1940. Oddly enough, it was designated Squadron Two as Squadron One was supposed to be assembled first, consisting as it did of the various boats built as a result of the motor torpedo boat design competition early in 1939. The training cruise of Squadron Two early in 1941, with green officers and crews, a minimum of spare parts and practically no basing, maintenance and repair facilities, was the first attempt of the Navy to see just what kind of boat these little ships were. Subjected to all manner of treatment, in-

One of the numerous Elco PT's recently built on the West Coast by the Harbor Boat Building Co. Kent Hitchcock Photo

cluding hurricanes and groundings, it actually proved that motor torpedo boats could go out and take it. That Squadron Three was able to carry out successful combat operations in the Philippines was due entirely to the courage, resourcefulness and ingenuity of the officers and men who manned them.

Owing to the combat experiences of Bulkeley, Kelly, Akers and Cox in the Philippines, many changes were made and the present boat represents a tremendous advance in both design and construction. But there were still in military circles many skeptics as to the real value of PT's even after Bulkeley's exploits. Operations in the Philippines were, of necessity, largely on a hit and run basis, and eventually all of his boats were destroyed. It was not until Squadron Four moved into Tulagi in October, 1942, that a plan of action was carried out and the enemy expelled from a definite position.

When the full story of Squadron Four in the Solomons during that October and the months which followed is finally written, it should prove to have been the turning point of motor torpedo boat strategy. Commander Alan Montgomery and his skippers and crew successfully repelled the large surface units of Tojo's navy and the efforts to dislodge the Marines from Guadalcanal contributed largely to the destruction of the Jap garrison. From Tulagi and Guadalcanal, PT's have now moved up through the other islands of the Solomon group, continually harassing enemy cruisers, destroyers and landing craft. In New Guinea, the same success has come to motor torpedo boat forces, and there is no question but that the confidential report of their activities in this vital area will prove that they are something much more than the "auxiliary" war craft originally conceived by many Naval minds.

In the Mediterranean sphere, where Mussolini boasted

*The plant of the Elco Naval Division employs the most modern boat-building technique. Left, bow view of the completed PT hull just prior to turning. Below, after the hulls have been turned over they move forward on the production line. Right, Rear Admiral J. M. Irish, Supervisor of Shipbuilding for the Third Naval District, and George Fulton, the plant's mechanical engineer, at the instrument board which controls the hull "turn over" mechanism. Elco Photos*

*Left, a deckhouse nearing completion. Above, the fo'c'sle looking forward. Right, looking aft in the "day room." A gun turret is on the port side. Elco Photos*

that his MAS's would "rule the roost," the British have successfully dominated the scene with many squadrons of PT's, several of which were built by the United States and transferred to them under Lend-Lease. Basing in Gibraltar at one end and at Alexandria at the other, the British MTB's worked along the North African coast in conjunction with the Allied armies until success brought them to the shores of Italy. In the landing at Sicily and in the Strait of Messina, the torpedo boats had "good hunting." A squadron of our boats finally joined the British units and gave an excellent account of themselves in the crossing of the Mediterranean.

Activities of motor torpedo boats in the Mediterranean are not as well known as are their exploits in the Pacific. They were not confined to torpedo tactics in this area but rather have been used in many ways with great success. Special reconnaissance work was performed off the Tunisian coast as well as the mining of the escape routes to Europe and the movement of commando details to critical areas. As mobile anti-aircraft batteries just off the shore, working along with the Army, they proved extremely successful. In fact, a whole new book of strategy for these little ships should evolve from their actions in the Mediterranean.

A chapter, quite unknown to the American public, was written by the Elco-built and British-manned boats at Tobruk when the Germans were driving the British back in their last rush to Egypt. A squadron was at anchor in the harbor when the alert commander, through his glasses, spotted some strange looking tanks creeping down the hills toward the own. Upon checking with G.H.Q., he was assured that these tanks were British, but another quick look proved them to be the vanguard of the Germans rolling in for the quick defeat of the garrison at Tobruk. Then ensued one of the most unusual actions in which PT boats have ever been engaged. A running battle between German tanks and British MTB's took place, with the little plywood craft

exchanging shots with the heavily armored land juggernauts. Several of the boats suffered direct hits and blew up but the others effectively laid a smoke screen, and not only covered the escape of a group of merchant vessels but also evacuated the British General Staff.

No summary of motor torpedo boat activities would be complete without a word about the British squadrons in the Channel and in the North Sea. In this rough and inclement area were born the first exploits of torpedo boats in this war. In September, 1939, the British had several types of these craft and there gradually developed a pattern which met with great success in slowing down the coastal convoys along the French and Netherlands coasts. Today, at least one squadron of American-built craft is being used by the British in this theater of operations. One of their great moments came when the German *Gneisenau*, *Scharnhorst* and *Prinz Eugen*, with a destroyer screen, forced the Channel to get back to German ports. The little boats drove home the attack, scoring a number of hits in extremely bad weather without much support.

If the lessons of combat are learned by our naval designers and boatbuilders, tomorrow's torpedo boat should be a versatile, hard-hitting craft suitable for offshore patrol, coastal defense, torpedo attack and anti-sub work. The development of light weight, rapid fire multiple mounts specially suited for fast, light displacement vessels should make the PT of the future a deadly weapon against any force attempting to invade our coastal areas or outlying posts. Properly coördinated with aircraft, torpedo boats should eventually take the place of many fixed coastal batteries, since their range far exceeds the limited arc of fire from stationary emplacements.

Undoubtedly, there will be many types and sizes of coastal defense craft and motor torpedo boats should play a leading

(Continued on page 46)

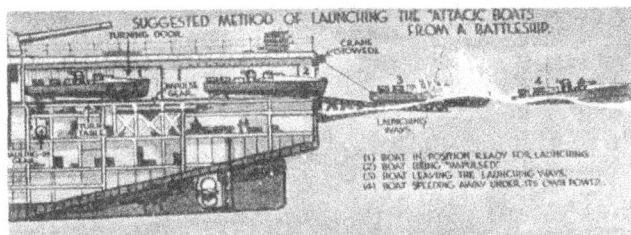

SUGGESTED METHOD OF LAUNCHING THE "ATTACK BOATS" FROM A BATTLESHIP.

(1) BOAT IN POSITION READY FOR LAUNCHING.
(2) BOAT BEING "CATAPULSED."
(3) BOAT LEAVING THE LAUNCHING WAYS.
(4) BOAT SPEEDING AWAY UNDER ITS OWN POWER.

*Above, an artist's conception of how battleship would be fitted to launch motor torpedo boats astern. London Illustrated News. Right, the plant's enclosed and steam-heated fitting out basin. Elco Photos*

# INSIGNIA
## OF THE
## PT SQUADRONS

At the inception of the motor torpedo boat program, Walt Disney created the now-famous insigne which was subsequently adopted as the symbol of the PT service. It shows a vengeful hornet astride a speeding torpedo, and it typifies the hell-for-leather spirit of all MTB men. As time went on, various squadrons devised their own individual insignia, some of the many which exist are shown here

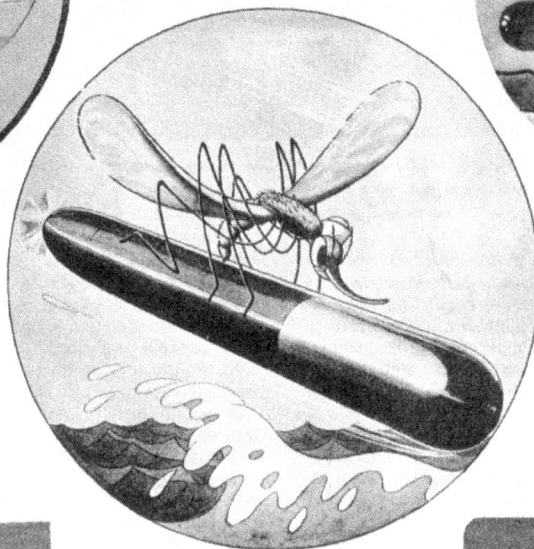

Endless days and nights of duty under fire create an indefinable attachment between the crews and their boats, and many of them have been given nicknames which are painted on their superstructures (see lower right). Typical of these names are "Green Beast," "Green Hornet," "Night Mare," "Miss Malaria," "Gremlin the Third" and "The Reluctant Dragon" — which always missed a fight!

Lower left, Lt. Comdr. Westholm and Commander Calvert proudly display the insigne of Flotilla One. The thirteen emblems of the rising sun indicate the number of Jap vessels which were destroyed by this one PT squadron. The combat records of other flotillas and squadrons are equally impressive, one boat, the "Green Hornet," is said to have sunk 920 times her weight in enemy surface craft. Life, Acme and U. S. Navy Photos

26

Along one of the streets of the MTB school at Melville, R. I., flanked by a row of Quonset huts, march the officer-students to their first morning class. Carroll van Ark Photo

# WHERE THEY LEARN TO BE TOUGH

### The Excellence of PT Officers and Crews Results from Intensified Training in the Specialized Duties of Their Service

#### By CRITCHELL RIMINGTON

"THE MISSION OF THE MOTOR TORPEDO BOAT SQUADRON TRAINING CENTER IS:

"To prepare and indoctrinate officers and enlisted personnel in the fundamentals of sound motor torpedo boat operations, maintenance and upkeep. The curriculum is arranged to accomplish this mission with a minimum of theory and classroom instruction and a maximum of practical work. Experience has indicated the necessity for adopting certain basic principles in training. These are, first, that each officer must be thoroughly trained in the particular duties of his rank or rate and, second, that he be trained in ratings on board of a PT vessel.

"COMMANDING OFFICER
*MTBS Training Center*"

TODAY, Mrs. Astor's horse has a lean and hungry look. Newport, but a few short years ago the summer playground of society's chosen few, has gone to war with a vengeance and what was once a quaint Colonial town of which the natives of Narragansett Bay were justly proud is now the post office address of countless vital naval establishments. The Navy's austere War College, once the largest group of buildings for miles around, is now dwarfed by an enormous "boot" camp where as many as 10,000 trainees are given a sound training in the rudiments of naval duties. Nearby, the Torpedo Station has mushroomed as if by magic. Some distance away from the din and bustle of Newport is Melville, long famous as the site of the Navy's huge net and fuel depot. Stretching along the Bay, this great shore base comprises a staggering assortment of buildings, tanks, cranes and docks through which roads and railway spurs are interlaced like an entangling spider web.

As is the case in all modern military or naval establishments, there is far more at Melville than meets the eye. Most of its installations are closely guarded military secrets but hidden away in one of the furthermost corners of the base is perhaps the most unusual naval training school in the United States: the Motor Torpedo Boat Squadron Training Center. Here, under the direction of its commanding officer, Lieut. Comdr. David J. Walsh, and many experienced PT officers with combat experience, the future captains and crews of the hard-hitting PT's are given a concentrated but

Left, a class of officers studies the fine points of piloting. Below, "light" exercise winds up a vigorous hour on the athletic field. Carroll van Ark and Official U. S. Navy Photos

27

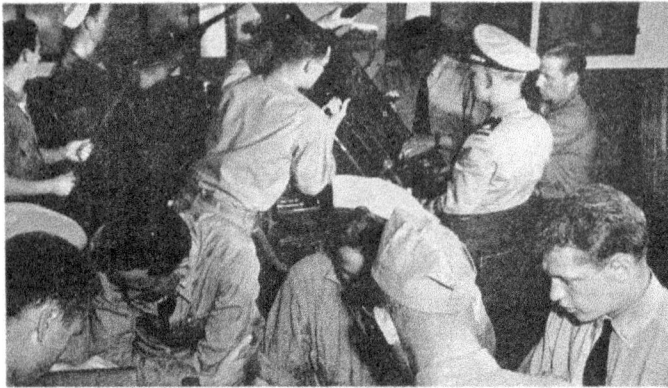

intensive training which provides them with the knowledge and stamina which enables them to use these small "vessels of opportunity" to a maximum degree of effectiveness. Established in the spring of 1942, its first skipper was Commander W. C. Specht, who, as Commanding Officer of Squadron One, directed the vigorous counter-attacking action of the PT's during the Japanese attack on Pearl Harbor. Architecturally speaking, the school is one of Spartan simplicity. Its buildings consist of row on row of Quonset huts set on narrow streets which run down to the basin where the PT's are based. These rugged little structures house classrooms, quarters and executive offices, and the sole means of distinguishing one from the other is by small and businesslike signs which indicate their purpose or occupants. The neatness and cleanliness associated with all naval establishments is everywhere evident, and all furniture and fittings are notable for their utter simplicity. The one bit of decoration is a miniature square of green which is appropriately named Bulkeley Park.

Operational practice decrees that all PT squadrons spend several months in a tropical climate far removed from the battlefront, during which time they receive the finishing touches in diversified operational experience and training which is so essential in the actual combat which follows. But, prior to this period, all officers and crews must go through a training school before being assigned to a PT squadron, and that school, "the PT Annapolis," is Melville. This training center, like numerous other specialized schools, is concerned with but one over all subject: the technique of PT operation.

How are future PT officers and enlisted personnel selected? In the first place, every PT man is a volunteer. Unlike the submarine service, which is also manned by volunteers, neither officers or crews receive extra pay for motor torpedo boat duty. Enlisted men are given the opportunity of volunteering while at a preliminary specialist school; later Melville calls for them. Officer candidates apply from the various Naval Reserve officer schools, and are there given a thorough interview to confirm their fitness for their chosen service. What with the success of the school and the increase in PT operation, Melville is today literally filled to capacity. Originally designed to handle approximately 40 officers and 200 enlisted men, today some 150 officers and 1000 enlisted men are taking its concentrated two months' course.

To volunteer for PT service, one must be between the ages of 20 and 34; at present, the age of the average student is somewhere between 24 and 25. The school's instructors make no bones about age qualifications. Younger men, they point out, are not apt to be as reliable as those in the middle twenties, and men over 35 are rarely able to stand the rigors of the service. Whereas a large percentage of Melville's students were star athletes in college, the curriculum requires brains as well as brawn, and the fact that a man was on an All American team does not necessarily mean that he will make a good PT officer.

The course of study includes seven basic subjects: combat tactics, engineering, gunnery, communications, navigation, ship and aircraft identification, and physical education. The school's fundamental idea is to train every man to do every other man's job. Hence, all courses include A, B and C classes in every subject. The A course is given to the specialist, the B course to the man most likely to fill his place if he should be injured in combat and the C

1, There are no parts of their weapons which PT men are not familiar with. 2, Ammunition is also the subject of exhaustive study. 3, The lethal wallop of the PT is aided by the Oerlikon (20 mm.) gun. 4, .50 cal. cartridges are deadly. OWI, Carroll van Ark, International News and U. S. Navy Photos

# Elco PTs

course provides a comprehensive coverage of the subject. Officers take the A and B courses in all subjects.

Lights go out at 11:00 p.m. for the officers and at 10:15 p.m. for the enlisted men — and woe to him who ignores Melville's rigid "blackout!" For officers, the length of the entire course is about eight and one-half weeks; for the enlisted men, the course is the same except for certain key ratings who have recently had their course increased to three months. Classes are purposely kept small. Every effort is made to give the men all the practical experience possible, and as much as 200 hours is spent in actual boat operation and maintenance. It is here that the most important work takes place since the term "boat operation" includes problems in navigation and piloting, gunnery, torpedo and depth charge practice, combat tactics, communications and the many problems of ship operation and maintenance. Many of the instructors in the practical courses are men who have had months of combat experience. These officers stay at Melville as instructors for about six months, thereafter they are assigned to new squadrons which are making up.

Physical exercise plays an important part in Melville's curriculum, and there is little doubt that the daily calisthenics on the drill field to the north of the school are long remembered by the future admirals who participated in them. To describe them as a "work out" is to be guilty of an understatement. A more accurate description was the comment of the school's physical director. "We give them hell," said he modestly.

In summarizing the school's program, Lieut. Comdr. Walsh said that "since the establishment of the MTBS Training Center at Melville, we have been engaged in a continuous series of development and experimental projects to improve the PT's combat efficiency. As might be imagined, this development work has involved gunnery, engineering, communications and general hull projects. Many of these projects have originated in the minds of the various officers attached to the staff, as well as from officers returning to this station from various combat areas. Suggestions have also been received from officers and men in the operating squadrons, and a majority of them have been acted upon. Furthermore, a great many recommendations have emanated from the various Bureaus of the Navy Department, who have sent representatives to Melville to witness and conduct various trials and tests. Our own officer staff here at the school, a majority of whom have had long experience with PT's, has also produced many improvements as well as new and original training aids for use by all departments. Much of our exploratory work is under the direction of our Lieut. J. W. Ewell, a veteran PT officer who has seen service at Pearl Harbor, Midway and in the Aleutians.

"In addition to the basic operational training, development and experimental work, Melville is also charged with the responsibility of conducting an intensive shakedown operations course for all MTB's built by the Electric Boat Company at Bayonne, N. J., and fitted out in the Brooklyn Navy Yard. These operations are identical with those conducted at Miami, and follow a syllabus which was drawn up by this command and approved by the Commander, Fleet Operational Training Command, U. S. Atlantic Fleet, who is the Type Commander of all MTB's, U. S. Atlantic Fleet, during the shakedown training period.

"These shakedown operations have proved of incalculable

(Continued on page 47)

*Three different types of motor torpedo boats are to be found at MTB training bases. 1, Two Elco PT's with student crews aboard. 2, A Higgins MTB on a night exercise at Miami. 3, A Huckins PT at full speed. 4, An instructor explains how a depth charge is "set." OWI, Huckins and U. S. Navy Photos*

# ELCO...GEARED AGAIN TO WAR

## Men Who Met 1915 U-Boat Menace with MLs Now Beat Plowshares of Peace Back into Weapons of War

*The men behind Elco's PT program. Left: Henry R. Sutphen, Executive Vice-President of the Electric Boat Company. Center: Preston L. Sutphen, Gen. Manager. Below: Irwin Chase, designer of the ML, now Managing Constructor, and his son, Commander Irwin Chase, Jr., USN.*

EIGHTY feet long, 19 knots speed, a 3-inch gun . . . those were the famous MLs, the Allies' successful answer to the U-Boats of the First World War. Many of them flew French, Italian and British flags but America built them — or, to be exact, Henry R. Sutphen conceived and planned them, Irwin Chase designed them, and the two of them together saw to it they were built in what is even today an amazing production record. . . . 550 MLs in 488 days.

That record makes clear why it is in no way surprising that, 25 years later, the Elco Naval Division is once more leading the way in PT Boat construction. Henry R. Sutphen, who in 1916 was manager of the Elco Works, is now executive vice-president of Elco's parent, the Electric Boat Company, and Irwin Chase, in 1916 a young designer with Elco, is at this writing the managing constructor of the Elco Naval Division.

The Elco Division is 52 years old this year. Its sister division, the Electro-Dynamic Works, responsible for much of the auxiliary electrical equipment in the Navy's big ships as well as the enormously complicated mechanisms that run the Navy's submarines, is even older, while the third part of the Electric Boat Company's triumvirate of operating divisions, the submarine works at Groton, Connecticut, largest privately owned submarine builder in this country, and now busy on a Navy order for scores of submarines, is almost as old itself.

The story of Elco is also the story of Mr. Sutphen, for he joined the company in 1892, immediately after its founding, and thus today is its oldest employee. Elco had its beginning in the Electric Launch Company, formed in 1892 to build for the Chicago World's Fair an order of fifty-five 36-foot electric launches for use on its lagoons. This project was successful, and the launches, if not quite as famous as Little Egypt, were certainly one of the Fair's most notable marvels.

Thus "launched," the company went ahead fast, and was responsible for a surprising number of innovations and improvements that today are taken for granted in the small-boat field, but at the time were truly pioneering adventures. Elco, for instance, built Hurrion, the first oil-electric yacht; it built the Auto-Boat, the first high-speed runabout. For the U. S. Life Saving Service, Elco designed and built the first self-righting, self-bailing, non-sinkable power lifeboat. Its principles are still standard. And for another government agency, the Revenue Service, Elco built the first gasoline cutter. There are many other milestones in Elco history, and a few deserve particular mention. Idealia, first Diesel Motor Yacht, was built by Elco in 1911. And the principle of the step hydroplane bottom was first incorporated in the Elco-plane. But what the company is proudest of, is its responsibility for introducing the principles of standardized construction to the small boat business, thus putting the sport of yachting within reach of an enormously increased public, and fostering the existence today of a healthy, thriving boat industry.

The Elco model that first put this production principle to practical use was developed in 1914, the 32-foot double cabin Elco Cruisette. Yachtsmen recognized her as one of the best small cruisers yet built, and she and her many prototypes became famous.

Then came the World War and Elco's amazing production of submarine chasers. How little they compare with the modern PTs turned out in Elco's new million-dollar Bayonne plant! Speeds are many times as great, armaments are incredibly more lethal, cruising ranges are ciphers apart. Yet many of the same personnel who made the old MLs possible are today helping to build Elco PTs.

Today general manager of Elco is P. L. Sutphen, son of H. R. Sutphen. A Princeton man, class of '21, and an army flier during the first World War, he joined the Electric Boat Company in 1922 at its Groton Plant, transferring to the Elco Division in 1929. From then until the present war work, he was responsible for the sales end of the business. Now as General Manager of both the Elco Yacht Division and the Elco Naval Division he sees to it that Elco's present war production lives up to its record of 1916.

Today, in fact, Electric Boat is a 100 per cent U. S. Navy concern. Submarines are built at Groton at an impressive rate; a huge volume of dynamos and electric equipment come from the Electro Dynamic Works at Bayonne, and while the actual production rate of Elco PTs must remain a Navy secret, its size would pain the Axis.

Naturally, no Elco motor yachts and cruisers are being built at present. But once this war is won, Elco will have a golden opportunity to resume private construction. Its plants and equipment are at the highest level they have ever been, and the experience and technical progress gained in PT construction will make possible many improvements in the design and building of the popular Elco Cruisettes.

*This article reprinted through the courtesy of MOTOR BOATING*

# *THE INSIDE STORY OF THE PTs

### Exploits of the Spectacular Motor Torpedo Boat in Battle Prove It a Mighty Weapon of Modern Warfare

### By WM. H. KOELBEL

THE world has suddenly become conscious of a powerful new weapon of war! Midget in size against the mammoth it destroys, it carries armament so deadly that the mightiest battleship is vulnerable to its lethal attack. Muffled engines drive it stealthily under cover of darkness into sure striking distance. Aboard the ship marked as its prey, there is no warning. Swiftly, suddenly, a torpedo finds its mark!

Too late, searchlights and guns swing into defensive action. As a crippled vessel plunges to the bottom, somewhere in the outer darkness thousands of horsepower roar into life. The attacker has vanished.

But the enemy knows that he has been the victim of surprise — another victim of the dreaded PT.

Small wonder that public imagination has been fired by the amazing exploits of these hard-hitting motor torpedo boats — motor boats that are making history in the Philippines, in the Mediterranean, in the English Channel, in the far-flung waters of the world.

True, duels between dreadnaughts on the high seas are dramatic. But when air waves crackle with news flashes of ship after ship succumbing to the raids of these elusive little hornets, it compels attention to the fact that the tremendous potentialities of the motor torpedo boat have already been conclusively proved.

### Lieut. Bulkeley Strikes the First Blow

No more thrilling episode will be recorded in the annals of modern warfare than the first audacious blow that Lieutenant John D. Bulkeley dealt the Japanese during the early weeks of the Philippine invasion, while American forces under command of General MacArthur held Bataan Peninsula against overwhelming odds.

This spectacular attack on a 5,000-ton Japanese vessel was brilliantly conceived, daringly executed. It was reported as the first exploit officially credited to any surface vessel in the Pacific theater of operations after consolidation of Allied naval command in the Southwestern Pacific under Admiral Hart. That it was only one of many such achievements that are destined to be recorded when the complete story of PT (Patrol Torpedo) action in this war has been told, is evidenced in other engagements which have followed closely on the heels of Lieut. Bulkeley's first epic foray.

Reconstructing the scene as pictured by the intrepid thirty-year-old squadron commander, we visualize him slipping out with two boats from the base where his squadron of hornets have their nest. In pitch darkness, he feels his way along the coast by skill born of training and instinct. His objective — Subic Bay on the West Coast of Luzon. Here enemy naval and auxiliary craft lie at anchor, in false security. Olongapo, naval substation, is in their possession, giving them, presumably, control of the bay, while net and boom defenses screen the approaches.

Engines throttled, Lieut. Bulkeley's craft steals in toward the inner harbor — to meet a storm of fire from batteries on both shores when his presence is finally detected.

In the darkness ahead loom up the indistinct outlines of an auxiliary cruiser, — a merchant ship armed with 6-inch guns, operating as a transport. Bulkeley pulls three throttles on his bridge. The responsive craft leaps into instantaneous action. At 40 knots he bears down on the doomed vessel, while startled enemy gun crews go hurriedly into action. The 3-inch shore batteries and machine guns spray a raking hail of lead as he lets go his torpedoes, jams the helm hard over, guns his three engines for their last ounce of power.

Before the enemy can get the range, Bulkeley has zig-zagged under wide-open throttle to safety — leaving consternation and destruction in his wake, while the Rising Sun of another Jap auxiliary cruiser is totally eclipsed in oily waters.

The communiqué's laconic comment: "This small boat carried out its difficult task while under fire of machine guns and three-inch shore batteries."

Today Lieut. Bulkeley, an Annapolis graduate of '33, wears the Distinguished Service Cross with oak cluster (equivalent to two Distinguished Service Crosses) as well as a Distinguished Conduct Star, Silver Star, and the Navy Cross for his feat. Fifty-seven members of his squadron have won 80 American decorations and four awards from the Philippine Commonwealth for the valor which has characterized all their exploits in the Philippines. Lieut. Bulkeley has seen service in the Navy's large surface craft, but his chosen field is with the PTs. As commander of a squadron of six boats, he has been in the Philippines for six months, proving repeatedly the great striking power of the motor torpedo boat.

The squadron of PTs that Lieut. Bulkeley has been using with such telling effect were built by the Elco Naval Division of the Electric Boat Company at Bayonne, New Jersey, now greatly expanded and seething with all-out production. Elsewhere in this issue is told the story of their development. How fast these PTs are rolling off the assembly lines is a military secret, but it can be said that mass production here is already a fact, not a fancy.

### Ensign Cox Repeats

The wires were scarcely cooled from carrying the news of Lieut.

*In night attack, PTs in the Philippines have repeatedly proved their great striking power*

Bulkeley's great achievement and the Japanese had not recovered from the surprise of the first assault when a second smashing blow was delivered by the torpedo boats of Bulkeley's squadron. Lieut. Bulkeley, Squadron Commander, with Ensign George Cox of Watertown, New York, at the helm of Bulkeley's flagship and Lieut. DeLong, Squadron Gunnery Officer, manning the torpedo director, sent torpedoes smashing into a second enemy vessel, repeating the first exploit again within a week.

Another enemy ship of 5,000 tons was marked for destruction — this time an aircraft tender carrying twenty planes. Again the target lay near Subic Bay off Sanpaloc Point. After the shock and first surprise, the enemy probably reasoned, quite erroneously, that General MacArthur's PTs would not dare a second raid under almost identical conditions.

Once more the harbor defenses were ineffectual in screening the PT from its prey. Additional 3-inch shore batteries had been placed on a hill to cover the approach to the enemy shipping lying within. Entangling nets had been laid across the entrance to the bay, strung with wire entanglements. Dodging through heavy shelling from shore batteries, through the nets almost into the shadow of the ships themselves straight into the machine gun fire of the enemy, PT-41 roared relentlessly on — her mission accomplished only when torpedoes from her tubes ripped gaping holes in the hull of the enemy vessel. On turning away from the enemy the shore batteries were engaged with the PT turrets pouring heavy raking machine gun fire into the batteries.

And the thrill of the evening came when PT-41 evaded one net by about ten feet on the starboard bow. Ensign Cox at the helm was the first one to sight the nets and by dexterous handling of the wheel avoided them.

During the exciting period while going through the nets Lieut. DeLong and Lieut. Bulkeley were busy discussing whether to return and fire more torpedoes into the enemy but, seeing the ship blowing up, her gasoline tanks apparently afire, they decided to save the remaining torpedoes.

After steaming five miles out to sea an attempt was made to stop the boat to watch the ship burning. By this time flames were shooting two and three hundred feet into the air from the spot where the ship had sunk beneath the surface. This was the gasoline burning on the surface.

Throttles were pulled back and they came back all the way, but the boat kept on. Immediately Ensign Cox rushed back to the engine room. He found the engineers had disconnected the throttle rods from the carburetors and were holding the levers against the carburetor stops by hand, evidently believing that they would get the most speed out of the boat in this manner. Needless to say the throttles were connected up again.

During this assignment PT-41 had been subjected to the heaviest shell fire experienced in the war, fragments from the shells coming as close as five and ten feet alongside the boat and ahead and astern of her. But not a single shell hit. In executing the midnight raid, Ensign Cox displayed the indomitable courage and alertness which had won for him the Croix de Guerre for service under fire with the American Volunteer Ambulance Corps serving with the French Army in 1940.

### Two Landing Barges Destroyed

Acting on orders to attack hostile shipping wherever found and to harass the enemy wherever they might be, it was Lieut. Bulkeley's practice to organize nightly patrols on which a small group of PTs under his command would patrol silently in total blackout or watch for enemy craft. Night operations gave him an overwhelming advantage over the more conspicuous enemy ships which he could then take by surprise. This was guerrilla warfare on the sea and Bulke-

*So fast and maneuverable are these Elco PTs that they are virtually impossible to hit. These are tremendous assets in modern warfare*

ley's band developed tactics entirely their own and suited to this type of war.

One night as he and Lieut. Kelly patrolled the Bataan coast in Stygian darkness a dark shape revealed the presence of an enemy craft. Lieut. Bulkeley with Lieut. Kelly at the wheel of PT-34 headed for it, creeping up at slow speed.

Suddenly a dark form materialized out of the inky blackness — scarcely a boat's length away. A party of 50 troops in an armored landing barge were attempting to make a landing beyond Lieutenant General Wainwright's lines on Bataan and Bulkeley had caught them before they had a chance to get ashore. The landing barge was diesel-powered and armored. As the Jap craft opened fire with four machine guns, Lieut. Bulkeley trained his guns on the barge and destroyed it under withering fire at point-blank range. All the Japanese troops were lost as the barge sank.

On the same patrol two hours later another landing barge was surprised returning from shore with three men aboard. This time Lieut. Bulkeley trained his guns on the vital spot beside the hull below the water line. As she sank, Lieut. Bulkeley leaped aboard alone, killed one Japanese who offered resistance and took two prisoners — a private and a captain. Both surrendered on their knees with hands in the air. Lieut. Bulkeley then set about to save these prisoners with the water rapidly pouring into the boat. Lieut. Kelly hoisted them aboard his boat and disarmed them. Private papers and dispatch cases were seized for their information, proving of utmost value to our forces.

## Warship Feels the PT's Sting

Communiqués from Corregidor carried news of a Japanese warship in Manila Bay on which two probable hits had been scored by a PT on patrol. Actually this encounter took place on the seaward side of Bataan Peninsula.

The Japanese cruiser, a ship of 6,000 tons, had been steaming through the night at 28 knots when Lieut. Bulkeley's PTs detected her. As the torpedo boat charged in to attack, the enemy ship trained powerful searchlights on her. Bulkeley's perilous course lay down a brilliantly illuminated path of light.

Facing a raking fire from the enemy's guns, Bulkeley closed in to a range where he could be certain that his torpedoes would count, and fired two. Both found their marks. Immediately the ship's speed dropped to 15 knots, then less.

Though communiqués at the time conservatively claimed only two probable hits, the next day this ship was reported beached 75 miles from Bataan and the Japanese were later said to be breaking her up for scrap.

The PT escaped without damage.

## Dive-Bombers Downed

For a time, there was a comparative lull in land operations in the Philippines. But the PTs were busy. Toward the end of January there was word in official communiqués of an unusual combat.

On this particular occasion two or three of Lieut. Bulkeley's boats were coming in from their nightly patrol. Dawn had already broken before they got back to their base. As they came into Manila Bay, two waves of enemy dive-bombers were seen approaching. Ignoring an opportunity to take cover against attack from the air, the PT's skipper opened his throttles and maneuvered to place his boat squarely in the line of flight of the second wave of approaching planes.

As they engaged the enemy, opening up with their .50-caliber machine guns, three of the planes were hit. This broke up the formation, driving them off, and when last seen

*(Continued on page 49)*

One of the famous MLs from World War I days. They saw plenty of action wherever the Allies had business to attend to

# FROM ML TO PT

It's a Far Cry from the Motor Launch of World War I to Today's Motor Torpedo Boat

By LAWRENCE CONANT

TIME: A dark night during the first World War. Place: Allied flying field near a town on the French coast. Captain Bogard, of the American air force, sets out in his Handley-Page on a bombing expedition. In the front gunpit is Claude Hope, a young lad from the British Naval Reserve. They've met a short while before, when off duty, and Claude is out for a lark before returning to his post.

Near as the Yanks can make out, Claude has no idea what war is like. About all he and his buddies from Eton and Harrow seem to do, day after day, is to tear around in bitty motor boats, crying "Beaver!" every time they spot a basket mast. Or maybe they just play tag, or convey "the captain's compliments." So Claude ("Flying? Find it jolly, eh?") is due for a ribbing, and a taste of the real thing.

He gets a thrill, all right, but not in just the way intended. When their objective is reached and, braving searchlight beams and anti-aircraft fire, they dive low to dump their deadly cargo, the boy up front leans far overside — he's lost his lunch, no doubt. Then the plane heads for home, and the boy is seen crawling toward the rear, shrieking in his thin, high voice; they catch the one word " . . . bomb!"

"Yes, bombs. We gave them hell! Get back — get back to your gun."

But for once no Huns give chase, and in due time Bogard

sets his plane down gently on the beach. "Oh, I say!" Claude marvels, climbing out. "Oh, I say, I shan't forget it! Tried to tell you, you know. . . ." And he points beneath the plane's right wing. There, its tip just touching the sand, dangles a live bomb that hung up when the release mechanism failed.

A few hours later Bogard keeps his promise to go for a ride with Claude in his water scooter — wouldn't do to disappoint the kid, who says he's eager to find a few more "beavers." "She sits right on top, you see," he comments as they start out. "Would float on a lawn, in a heavy dew. Goes right over them like a bit of paper." (That the "them" refers to mines, Claude doesn't say.)

But why the machine gun swiveled at the stern? And why that low screen with its single forward-staring eye? And what's Muriel for — that overgrown, half-buried fountain pen on which Bogard sits astride? His face grows sober, thoughtful, and he buttons his trench coat closer, as though he's getting cold.

Does all this have a familiar ring to you? It should, for it's a résumé (up to a point) of one of the best war-exploit stories ever written. If you remember William Faulkner's "Turn About," you'll know that Bogard, hardened though he is to danger, gets the thrill of *his* young life, out there on Claude's

*This article reprinted through the courtesy of Motor Boating*

frail motor torpedo boat. If you haven't read it, you have a treat in store which we don't propose to spoil. . . .

Fiction, but it's based on fact. Claude's CMB (coastal motor boat, or "hush boat") had its sisters and half-sisters by the score — mostly 40- and 55-foot Thornycrofts carrying a Lewis gun and a stern-launched torpedo. Even more useful were the somewhat larger MLs (motor launches), with depth-bomb racks and twin Standard motors, which Britain and its Allies employed with telling effect against German U-boats and for many other inshore operations, both offensive and defensive. Credit for these history-making craft goes to Elco, the boat-building firm of Bayonne, N. J., a firm whose name crops up repeatedly in these pages, and for good reason. The ML venture called for equal parts of enterprise, ingenuity, and vision. That was in the best American tradition. So was the fact that the end product shattered tradition, and was better than anyone had a right to expect.

One day in 1913 a man who started with the firm as office boy was showing a father and son through the Elco plant. He didn't quite catch the name, but they said "We're from Detroit." As the man seemed to know something of motors, the talk turned to mass production. "Some day, perhaps," said their escort, "we'll be building boats on an assembly line, the way they turn out autos where you come from."

"No, you never will," was the quick response. "Too much handwork involved."

A few minutes later the visitor said he'd buy a 36-foot electric launch, sight of which had made his son's eyes sparkle. He handed over a check signed "Henry Ford."

Soon the first World War broke out. Toward the last, Ford was building 200-foot steel-hulled subchasers, but they never saw active service. Meantime Henry R. Sutphen, the man to whom he'd said "It can't be done," had beaten him to it with a fleet of 722 smaller craft for the navies of England, America, Italy and France. Five hundred and fifty of these 80-foot MLs left their cradles in 488 days; and that, in the boat-building industry, is mass production or the next thing to it.

The Elco boats came almost as the answer to a prayer — indeed, we suspect that "almost" could drop out. For in the spring of 1915 the British Admiralty was getting desperate. German U-boats were raising hob with shipping, and all the King's Navy couldn't turn the tide. A special commission of engineers was rushed to America, where the tin shark was born, to enlist help in putting it to rout. They turned to Elco — naturally enough, for ever since 1893, when the company turned out 50 electric launches for the Chicago World's Fair, it had made a specialty of standardized boats which did its reputation proud.

Even so, the problem they put up to Irwin Chase, Elco designer, was something of a poser. Structural engineers who were consulted declined to tackle the project. It called for an

*One small group of World War I MLs from a total of 550 of these 80 footers which Elco produced, ready for service, in 488 days*

*A squadron of Elco PTs, so vastly superior to the old ML as to leave little opportunity for comparisons. Elco has proved that they can be turned out by mass production methods*

© M. Rosenfeld

unheard-of combination of quantity production and individual performance: speed 19 knots *minimum*, even in dirty weather (as against the accepted 15 for boats of this size and type), full-speed cruising radius 800 miles (2,000 gallons of gas, please), dead weight 20,000 pounds . . . oh yes, and the craft must be able to maintain station come hell or high water, or both. As Henry Ford had intimated, boats are something else again when it comes to mass production; but Messrs. Sutphen and Chase were able to deliver on all counts, besides a few the British hadn't thought of. And it was all done in jig time, with jigs being used to best advantage.

To the Dover Patrol, Elco's MLs were a godsend, even though their round bottoms rolled far too much to make rough-weather traveling a pleasure cruise, and the best cast-iron stomach refused to stay put. The Elco "movies" criss-crossed the English Channel, dashed about like water bugs on the North Sea, playing David and Goliath. They patrolled for submarines, yes; left ashcans on their doorsteps in lieu of calling cards. *And* laid mines, swept mines with the D sweep or the treacherous Q-type paravanes, convoyed merchant vessels, rescued seaplane crews — all without listening devices or wireless sets, left alone a wireless telephone. By the time they'd been dubbed the Mosquito Fleet they'd seen service, too, in the Mediterranean, at the Dardanelles, and in the Adriatic. But to say that they "saw service" is not the half of it.

You've heard about Zeebrugge, and how on St. George's Day, 1918, in the space of 100 minutes after the first shot was fired, two concrete-laden blockships choked the mouth of the canal which the Germans had been using as a base for

submarines. And no doubt you're familiar with the part the MLs played: how they laid a smoke screen for the British flotilla when airplanes discovered its approach that historic night, only to see the enemy send up star shells that give the volunteer invaders a "very naked feeling," as one of them put it later . . . how, despite a battery of searchlights and an inferno of gunfire from both sides, the MLs led the way through a gap that had been blasted in the Mole, set off flares to guide the blockships in, stood by to pick up the crews . . . how one ML, with a normal complement of ten, took aboard more than a hundred survivors and, after running a gantlet of machine-gun fire as it hugged the Mole wall to escape being hit by shrapnel and pom-pom shells, made for the Channel and home . . . how only two MLs out of 33 were lost.

But perhaps you haven't heard about the payoff: it came when six MLs converged on Dover Harbor out of the mist and saw that *H.M.S.* Vindictive, still licking its wounds, had preceded them. The men who thronged her decks — remnants of the landing party in addition to the crew — lined up to wave their caps and cheer as the MLs slowly passed. Heroes all, they knew a hero when they saw one!

On that same night of April 22–23 an obortive attempt was made at Ostend to block the other end of the Bruges Canal, and on May 9 the Britishers had a more successful go at it. Again the cruiser Vindictive and the MLs worked in unison. This time it was Vindictive's turn to be scuttled for the cause, but Elco's MLs were close at hand to take on all survivors.

The Royal Naval Volunteer Reserve had no monopoly on motor boat exploits, however. Even the Germans had their

© M. Rosenfeld

*Above: PT 10, first of a fleet of Elco motor torpedo boats, typifying one of the motor boat industry's chief contributions in supplying modern weapons of war. Below: Secretary of the Navy Knox (top center) inspects a PT with Navy officials and Elco executives*

© M. Rosenfeld

PMBs, though these were no great shucks, either in speed or in effectiveness. France went in for both single-step hydroplanes (VTBs) and V-bottom Aeromarines. Italy, which in those days seemed to know on which side her bread was buttered, had her Motobarche Anti-Sommergibili — MAS for short. These initials inspired the poet d'Annunzio to supply a Latin motto, Memento Audare Sempre (remember always to dare), and the men who manned the pint-sized fleet did a good job of "remembering."

In June 1918 they attacked an Austrian squadron headed for Cattaro. One Rizzo, traveling at low speed so that his wake would not attract attention, succeeded in sinking the dreadnaught Svent Istvan (St. Stephen). Turning tail, the Austrians steamed back to Pola, where they were still holed up October 31. So the Italian mosquitoes came scooting right into the harbor; and there Signor Paolucci, employing a makeshift controllable mine, blew up the battleship Viribus Unitis, together with a Yugoslav admiral and the crew.

Motor boats also scored an outstanding success in the summer of 1919, in raids on Kronstadt which came as an aftermath of the Russian Revolution. Two capital ships, a cruiser and a brace of destroyers were among the craft sunk or disabled, while only two mosquitoes — count them, one, two — failed to return. And on August 10 of the previous fall came an action which presaged developments of the present World War. Six British CMBs were put out of action by German planes, but it took eight of them to turn the trick.

Small wonder that in the lull between two wars, the navies of the world continued to toy with a class of fighting craft which, thanks primarily to Elco, had proved anything but toys!

"Motor Boating" has treated these various designs at some length in past issues (notably August 1940). Suffice it to say here that more than a dozen nations experimented with step hydroplanes and V-bottoms; with torpedo tubes that rode amidships and torpedoes that were fired from a trough in the stern; with a combination of torpedoes and depth charges; with machine and anti-aircraft guns, and even with small cannon.

The movement got under way in earnest in the early '30's, when improved models of the Italian MAS were forthcoming. In England the bulk of experimental work has been done by Vosper, Thornycroft, and Hubert Scott-Paine of the

*(Continued on page 53)*

# MILESTONES IN

## 50 Years of Experience In Standardized Boat Building Produced the World's Fastest Combat Vessel

**1893** . . . Thousands of sightseers at the Columbian Exposition of the original Chicago World's Fair were thrilled by rides in electric launches like this — the granddaddy of future Elcos.

**1911** . . . Hold your hats, folks. It's the sensational Elcoplane! This 20-foot speedster was guaranteed to do 35 m.p.h. One owner wrote "As for sport — it has everything else beat, on earth or in the air."

**1914** . . . This 75 horsepower Elco Express was the forerunner of the modern de luxe runabout. Built entirely of solid mahogany. Speed, 24 m.p.h.

# Elco HISTORY

**1915** . . . Over seven hundred of these 80-foot subchasers, known as MLs, were built by Elco for Great Britain, France and Italy during World War I.

**1927** . . . Famous as the "Home Afloat," the Elco Cruisette was the first standardized cruiser. It achieved worldwide popularity as a result of highly desirable features it offered at a reasonable price.

**1938** . . . This fine Elco 44 shows the ultimate development in the Cruisette before the war. This "ideal boat," based on the experience of hundreds of yachtsmen who specified what features they most desired and the space they wanted for this and that.

**1943** . . . U.S.S. PT 117. Eighty feet of fighting fury and every inch an Elco! Its achievements on many naval battle fronts are making history. Its performance and stamina have set a standard which will have a profound effect on boats of the future.

# VICTORY will bring

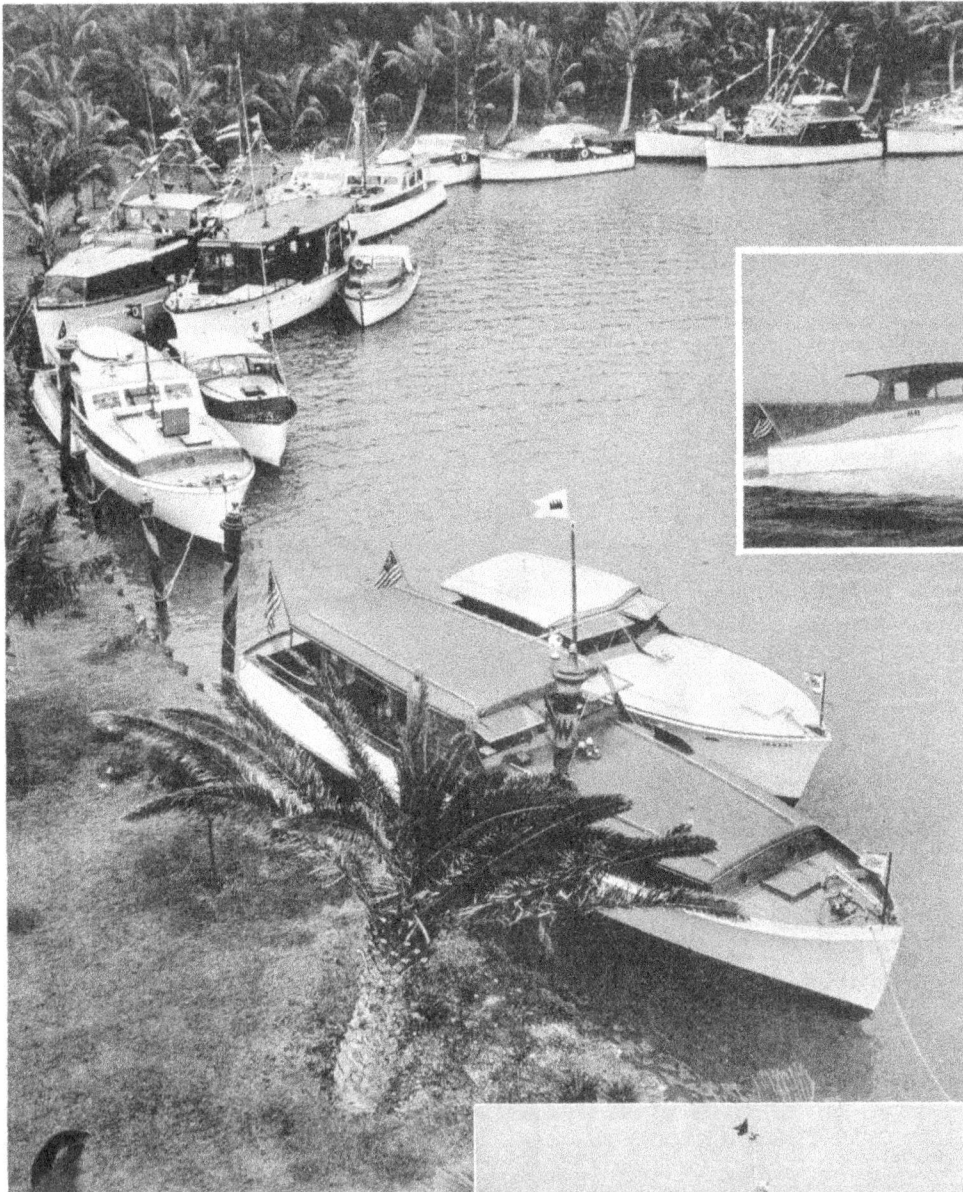

ELCOETTE — 32' . . . Fast, compact Sport Cruiser. Speed, 23 m.p.h. Sleeps 4 or 5. Ideal for sport fishing.

ELCOs are prominently represented in this gathering of pre-war cruisers at Miami.

ELCO — 57' . . . Brilliantly designed, superbly built Motor Yacht, developed from the famous Elco 53 and providing a new standard of comfort and luxury for a boat of its size.

# them back

THESE peacetime cruisers exemplify the leadership in boatbuilding achieved by Elco before the war.

Today, this leadership is reflected in the sleek lines, flashing performance and sound construction of Elco PTs — the world's fastest combat vessels.

Tomorrow, when victory is won, the new Elco pleasure craft will offer many advancements resulting from new designs, new materials and revolutionary boatbuilding methods developed for PT production.

*ELCO — 53' . . . A fine Motor Yacht whose graceful flowing lines and superb proportions mark her instantly as a seagoing aristocrat.*

*ELCO — 44' Special . . . There's a hint of the Elcos of the future in this sleek, streamlined, custom-built version of the Elco 44 Cruisette.*

## "GREEN DRAGONS" OF NEW GUINEA

Because of their relatively small size, PTs can be based in the many rivers and inlets that abound in the tropic island groups. Screened by overhanging trees and the camouflage they have added, the PT Squadrons live in comparative ease at the bases they have hewn out of the "gumbo" soil. Boats from such bases participated in the campaign which crumbled the Japanese bastion at Lae.

Top, looking reptilian in its disguise, this Elco PT blends into the jungle background. Upper left, under overhanging camouflage nets, crews get a brief respite. Lower left, drums of fuel are rolled off the ramp of an LCM. Bottom, four abreast to a river "hitching post" in the oily waters of a hidden New Guinea anchorage. Official U. S. Navy Photos

*Modern wartime
production line*

L MACINTYRE

## PT'S IN THE PACIFIC

*(Continued from page 18)*

stop short of the deck planking. Otherwise, his seagoing career would have been terminated earlier than it was. "PT" couldn't stay at sea long, anyway. The salt spray caused his eyes to develop myopia or the squirrel equivalent. So "PT" was beached and joined the assortment of pets on the base which were as varied as their masters' imaginations. The densely populated jungle provided an unlimited supply.

The greatest pet of all, though, was human. There were two of them — Navy "chiefs" who were the warp and woof of the repair facilities at the base and who could perform maintenance miracles that kept the boats going in spite of hidden reefs, Jap shells, and the usual hull and engine casualties resulting from constant patrols and action. Holes would be patched with copper plate, propellers would be hammered back into shape with a mallet and a blowtorch. And what they and their henchmen could do with baling wire would fill a technical manual. They even constructed a marine railway whose power was as primitive as its gear — natives on a winch and cable. The two "chiefs" and their gangs stayed ashore and, because of them, the PT's stayed afloat and the boats' personnel had occasion to be profoundly grateful for this support at the base.

Without the maintenance gang, the lieutenant's boat never would have been so successful in the action against the landing barges. That action was tough going and consisted of slambang infighting that only 100 yards of bullet-covered water kept from being hand to hand. The prize was four landing barges. Each carried more than 100 men and each bristled like a porcupine with machine guns. Altogether a formidable force in shallow water.

The lieutenant's boat came upon the scene purely by chance, at the end of a deadly dull night patrol. A lone PT *versus* four heavily armed barges. Not exactly an even match, but the solitary PT moved in to the attack, and so close did she carry her runs on the barges that they threatened to be swamped by the wake. The engagement lasted a long 30 minutes and casualties amongst the Japs were heavy from the fire of the PT's guns. All of the latter were constantly barking and they were augmented by tommy guns and .45's. The opposing fire, even an explosive shell that burst through the hull below the forecastle, failed to stop the PT. Net result: three barges sunk, one left burning. Personnel losses great.

The next loss of Jap barges in which his PT made an assist was not only heavy in personnel but in barges, too. Six of them. Six landing barges that,

in the dark, made the fatal mistake of throwing their lines across the PT and mooring to her. The Skipper of the PT, after recovering from his amazement at this unconscious audacity, emptied a tommy gun at the equally stunned Nips, roused his crew, cleared the lines of the barges, stood clear of them and, with the help of nearby PT's, sank all six of the barges.

Then there was that ghastly night when the lieutenant won his Navy Cross and his best friend had lost his life. By that time, he was Skipper of his own boat, and his friend the Skipper of another. Together, they had passed through a half year of battle experience, of jungle duty, of action, of inaction and of high excitement. They knew, and thoroughly understood, the technique of PT fighting and their crews knew it, too. Men and officers had been hardened under fire and welded into an efficient fighting unit. They were serving in one of the smallest Navy units afloat: a boat that is light and fragile and speedy — but also heavy with the power to sink craft many times her size.

The two of them, the lieutenant and his friend, went out alone to intercept Japanese "tin cans" off the island. Only the lieutenant came back and this was the brief action report he turned in: "As we went to intercept the Jap destroyers, enemy planes were trying to spot us. That meant for sure the 'cans' were coming. Planes came first and they bombed us, but my gunners threw everything at them that wasn't secured. I don't know how much damage we did to them; all they did to us was to shoot off the antenna a foot above the cockpit and too close for comfort to my left ear.

"A bit later, we sighted a destroyer, two, three — four of them. We headed directly for them and at 900 yards fired two 'fish' that missed and two that found their marks. The results were as terrifying as they were gratifying. It's a beautiful sight when enemy ships blow up. But it frightens you.

"We turned to retire and then a searchlight caught us. The first salvo was 200 yards over, the second 30 yards short, and the third blew a hole in our bow. Our speed was not affected and, by keeping the engines going their limit, we lifted the hole in the bow clear of the water and beached ourselves on a friendly island. Smoke covered our retreat but did not conceal a burst of flame on our starboard quarter. I hoped it was an enemy ship, but I was wrong. It was my friend's boat. He wasn't as lucky as I was. He didn't make the beach."

*The opinions or assertions contained herein are the private ones
of the writer and are not to be construed as official or reflecting
the views of the Navy Department or the Naval Service at large.*

# THE DEVELOPMENT OF THE PT

(Continued from page 4)

the attacks on Zeebrugge and Ostend in April, 1918. Their main task was laying smoke buoys in advanced positions and smoke screens around the harbor entrance by using chlor-sulphonic acid in their exhausts. Routine duties of CMB's were mine laying, rescue of crews from fallen planes, and patrol off the Belgian Coast. In one action, six CMB's were attacked by eight German aircraft and all the boats were temporarily put out of commission though none were lost. Motor torpedo boats were also used extensively in the raids on Kronstadt after the Russian revolution. In these most spectacular operations, two capital ships, a cruiser, two destroyers and other craft were sunk or completely disabled while only two CMB's were lost (probably by mines). The results achieved by both the British and Italian boats formed the first basis to substantiate the claims of the supporters of these vessels, and must be considered responsible for the early adoption of this type of craft by nearly every navy.

As a result of the British CMB, Germany built boats known as patrol motor boats (PMB's). Based in the harbor of Blankenberghe, they were both slow and ineffective. The design and performance of German motor torpedo boats have shown such remarkable improvements in this war that their accomplishments are worthy of mention. Before and since the battle of France, Germany had used a fast armored vessel known as the "E" boat. They have many practical uses such as attacks against convoys, escort duty, mine laying and the rescue of plane pilots. Boats of this type range in length from 80 to 110 feet, are about 65 tons displacement and have a speed of about 30 to 36 knots. They carry from two to four torpedo tubes, several heavy machine guns, and some armor. Seaworthy and capable of taking considerable punishment, they are equipped with Diesel engines that have proven satisfactory. At first, the British held the "E" boats in contempt but, when the latter started operating in packs and disrupting British channel traffic, the British began earnestly to improve their own craft and to use motor gunboats in combating those of the enemy. Motor gunboats, incidentally, are MTB's that have had the tubes removed and more and heavier guns added, thus increasing their fire power.

The first spark of motor torpedo boat enthusiasm in this country probably resulted from the interest in the establishment of a volunteer patrol squadron of small boats in the first World War. President Roosevelt, then Assistant Secretary of the Navy, took an active interest in patrol craft and persuaded A. Loring Swasey, now a Naval Reserve Captain in the Patrol Craft section of the Bureau of Ships, to build five volunteer sub-chasers. These and many others did considerable patrol work and established an excellent combat record.

Our early destroyers were little more than torpedo boats. They were small in size, carried torpedoes and light additional armament. Then came a gradual increase in size to 1200 tons and, later, they were stepped up to 1500 and 1850 tons. While present day destroyers increased to a size of 2100 and 2250 tons, and the entire tempo of warship construction was tuned to make the large and heavy type ships larger and heavier, there still remains the need for the fast small craft which can carry and deliver a heavy punch. The 80-foot sub-chasers (ML's) which were built for Britain in great quantities in the last war by The Electric Boat Co. also inspired an interest in the motor launch and coastal motor torpedo boat as used by Britain. Soon after the first World War, the Navy Department bought both a 40- and a 50-foot British Thornycroft boat for testing purposes, but no further progress was made with the development of such boats until 1937.

General Douglas MacArthur, upon appointment to organize and build up the Filipino Army, became cognizant of the ever threatening dangers from Japanese aggression and the rôle that small, fast motor torpedo boats might play in strengthening the Islands' defenses. He reasoned that the motor torpedo boat might provide a solution, as she could be built in a hurry at a minimum cost, and at the same time, in conjunction with aircraft, provide the Philippines with a good defensive and striking force. In this interest, he journeyed back to the United States to press his program for defense. In the United States, remote from any apparent danger, he found few with enthusiasm for such craft, so he appealed to his old friend Admiral Leahy, then Chief of Naval Operations, to plead his dire need of 100 small, fast boats to defend the Philippine Islands. The final and indirect outcome of this appeal was a $15,000,000 appropriation put through Congress for the development of such craft.

Thereafter, the early designs were developed without a specific employment plan in mind. One faction maintained that the size of the boat should be kept down, so that the target presented would be negligible. Another faction declared that the boats should be larger to increase their seaworthiness. A third insisted on the construction of torpedo boat catchers in an effort to counteract the effect of the motor torpedo boats being built by potential enemy countries, while the fourth held that, since the small

boats could not remain at sea for any length of time and the cruising radius would be short, there would be no need for motor torpedo boat catchers as there would be nothing for them to catch. Still another claimed it was foolish to spend $200,000 to $300,000 for such a boat when a torpedo plane, costing about the same amount, could carry a torpedo much faster and further and probably be more effective. The PT proponents replied by stating that the type of weather that would normally ground aircraft — darkness, fog and low visibility — would prove ideal for PT operation and, besides, the boats could remain at sea longer than aircraft could remain in the air. The result was a compromise in design.

Thereafter the development of the PT was marked by a design contest, open to civilian naval architects, and by the further development of the types of PT's which are now a part of the United States battle fleet. For the record, it is interesting to note that one of the original Navy contracts provided for the construction of PTC's (Patrol Torpedo Boat Chasers). The difference between the PT's and the PTC's was only a matter of armament and equipment. Instead of carrying four torpedoes, the first PTC's carried about 22 depth charges in racks, and two Y guns aft. Subsequently, the construction of this type of boat was discontinued. PT's 10 to 19 were fitted with 18" torpedo tubes; PTC's 1 to 12 were rated as subchasers.

By July, 1941, PT's 20 to 48 were completed by the Naval Division of The Electric Boat Co. and delivered to the U. S. Navy. They were commissioned as the second motor torpedo boat Squadrons One and Two. In addition to the four 21" torpedoes, these vessels were armed with two twin 50 cal. machine guns mounted in two power-driven turrets. The crews for each were two officers and eight men.

About this time, three Elco 77-foot boats from Squadron One, and Three from Squadron Two were selected and commissioned as Squadron Three, were loaded aboard a tanker and shipped to the Philippines where they arrived in October, 1941. A few weeks later, Squadron One, consisting of twelve Elco-built PT's under the command of Lieutenant Commander W. C. Specht, U. S. N., were shipped to Pearl Harbor where they arrived the latter part of August, 1941. Shortly after the outbreak of war on December 7th, 1941, motor torpedo boat Squadron Two, consisting of eleven Elco-built PT's, were transported to Panama in the same manner.

The PT's now in operation range from 77 to 80 feet in length, have three 1350 hp. engines with a full load speed in excess of 40 knots, with either four torpedo tubes or two torpedo tubes and eight depth charges or four mine racks, two .50 caliber machine guns, a 20 mm. gun and a smoke screen generator. Each boat carries a complement of eleven, two officers and nine men.

The primary mission of motor torpedo boats is to attack enemy surface vessels. Their high speed, handiness and torpedo armament make them most suitable for surprise attacks against enemy surface vessels at night or during low visibility. The secondary missions which they may be called upon at times to fulfill are:

(a) Anti-submarine operations;
(b) Emergency rescue vessels;
(c) Escort duty;
(d) Mine laying;
(e) Commando Missions.

We must remember that motor torpedo boats, like aircraft, are not a "cure all" and their employment for other purposes than those for which they are designed tends to reduce their life and effectiveness when called upon to fulfill their primary mission. Uses such as picket duty, anti-submarine patrol and as high speed transports place unnecessary hours of duty on the engines and other equipment, thereby reducing the boats' efficiency.

Motor torpedo boats, like aircraft, require experienced and qualified operating personnel, adequate base and tender repair facilities and expert ground and servicing crews. Any provisions short of this are inadequate, as the requirements of constant upkeep of hulls, machinery and armament are the greatest obstacles to proper and effective operation. This fact has been recognized by the Navy since the war, and the Navy has now established PT bases in various theaters of operations. In addition, large motor torpedo boat tenders are now in service which constitute mobile advance bases. These ships facilitate moving PT's into any occupied area with the first landing groups and also permit them to operate offensively and defensively and be partially serviced before their main base equipment and supplies are moved up. It may be expected that the PT's, like the Marines, will be the first vessels to arrive at any front.

The normal motor torpedo boat squadron consists of eight to twelve boats and a complement of about 25 officers and 175 enlisted personnel. Besides the boat crews, each squadron has additional personnel for base administration, maintenance, overhaul and upkeep. Each boat has a crew's compartment forward capable of billeting eight men and two small staterooms for officers. There is also a small galley. Boats can operate away from tender or base for many hours for which full rations are carried; emergency rations carried permit subsistence for a day or two longer. In combat areas, where speed is vitally important, all excess equipment such as bunks, cooking gear, etc., is removed to cut down weight and help increase speed. Sandwiches and vacuum jugs of coffee usually provide all the sustenance when boats are operating on a mission.

Considerable publicity has given the impression that our motor torpedo boats are capable of fantastic speeds. Our present boats are a compromise between speed, seaworthiness, armament and being self-sustaining. Their main defensive power lies in small size, speed, handiness, ability to lay smoke screens and to cruise silently at low speed.

_The opinions or assertions contained herein are the private ones of the writers and are not to be construed as official or reflecting the views of the Navy or the Naval service at large._

## THE STORY BEHIND "THE EXPENDABLES"

_(Continued from page 22)_

at least four different ways: 1. The tendency to bury the stem head and ship seas on deck has been overcome by a tremendously buoyant bow which rises quickly to clear the oncoming crest. 2. The sharp deadrise and calculated shape of the chines forward have eliminated the destructive pounding so characteristic of many V-bottom hull forms when going to windward. 3. The hull lines aft, with flaring sides, good deadrise and narrow stern, have cured the tendency to broach to which has been the curse of so many fast power boats and, 4. The great stability of the hull, with the anti-roll chocks on the chines, makes the boats quite comfortable even when lying in the trough of the sea. While the roll may be quick, it seldom exceeds 10° and all previous theories of optimum metacentric heights for seaworthiness had to be revised as the boats have proved popular with even the "poor sailors."

While on this subject, I cannot give too much credit to the Navy Department for the many suggestions which have contributed so much to the PT's seaworthiness and reliability. From the Bureau of Ships, the PT school at Melville and from countless naval officers at sea, has come a steady stream of ideas of many kinds which have collectively done much to improve the boats' design and performance. Also, we were most fortunate in having the assistance of our associate organization, The Electric Boat Company of New London. Its naval architects, marine, electrical and ordnance engineers are responsible for the ingenuity and speed with which hundreds of problems were solved in the first boats which we built.

One of the most interesting aspects of perfecting the design of the small, high speed boat is that it requires constant exploration. Little data are on record, and what there are often prove to be incorrect. In the case of Elco PT's, we have had, with the encouragement of our Navy, a unique opportunity to carry on a most extensive series of experiments without delaying our regular contract trials. (Every boat to date has been delivered ahead of contract time and exceeded all performance guarantees.) Literally thousands of trials have been run on hundreds of boats and complete records of every minute's running have been kept with exceptional accuracy. For each run over the measured course, we have recorded over 40 different readings — including some unusual items such as manifold pressures, change of trim, position of bow wave, helm angle, accelerations (vertical) and relative air speed. Some of our special trials have investigated the following: modification of hull lines, strength of structures, propellers (30 designs), maneuvering with rudders, fins and engines, windage, underbody fouling, displacement effect on speed and horse power, radius of action, shoal water effects, trim (effect on resistance and seaworthiness), seaworthiness (pitch, roll, pounding and spray), stability (static and dynamic), vibration, scoops and fittings, camouflage, rise of the center of gravity under way, ordnance (torpedo tubes, gun mounts, smoke, etc.), communications, anchors, towing and being towed, black-out and night lighting, and mufflers. We feel that these experiments have paid big dividends in resulting improvements, making it possible to carry almost double the original "pay load" over twice the original radius of action and with more speed, maneuverability, seaworthiness and strength.

Some of the curious things we have discovered may have no immediate practical value but are none the less interesting. They could, perhaps, form a basis for a PT Quiz, for instance: Why does an Elco PT under way always heel to windward? How can a PT have _two_ speeds differing by as much as 2½ knots at the _same_ r.p.m., all conditions of boat and trial course being absolutely identical? I wonder how many yachtsmen can answer these correctly?

The big and ever-present problems in PT design are saving weight and reducing construction time. The coöperation we have received from all of our suppliers has been of incalculable aid in this connection. Not only have we benefited by the "know how" of well-known corporations such as Aluminum Co. of America, which with us designed the fuel tanks which are bigger and lighter than are to be found on any plane; International Nickel, which has made the remarkable Monel shafts; and the U. S. Plywood prod-

ucts, which have saved hundreds of pounds and thousands of hours, but also by the coöperation of dozens of other firms whose people have been inspired by the exploits of "The Expendables."

In many respects, the modern PT is more like a plane than a boat and, therefore, needs the same degree of maintenance as does a plane. And, in the same way that a squadron of aircraft would never be sent into operation without the necessary ground and maintenance crews, so is it equally impractical to send a PT squadron into combat without adequate facilities for its constant care. The Navy is among the first to realize that this all-important consideration was overlooked at the beginning of hostilities, and it is astonishing that the original squadrons were able to operate as long as they did without them. Today, the picture is a different one; special types of mother ships and highly trained ship- and shore-based maintenance crews are now an essential part of every combat unit.

At best, prophecy is dangerous. One man's guess as to the future development of the PT is as good as another's. But we at Elco need no crystal ball to foresee the possibilities for the future development of the motor torpedo boat. Experiments have shown that, even in these first years of PT construction, we have introduced new materials, new techniques and a new conception of the potentialities of the internal combustion engine. Even now, we have greatly improved the PT's performance. In something less than three years, we have cut construction time in half. These are but a few of the tangibles; the intangibles are legion.

There will always be different opinions as to the ideal size of the motor torpedo boat yet I cannot see any legitimate reason for any substantial increase in their water line length. The characteristics of modern warfare indicate that one of the PT's principal adversaries will always be the airplane, and it therefore follows that the size and performance characteristics of one will always have a great effect on those of the other.

But, whatever their size or design, they are a type of war craft which still has the future before it. While I am proud indeed of the job that the Elco organization has done, and I wish that I could name and thank publicly all of them who so richly deserve the highest praise, I am very much aware that a PT is, after all, only another boat and it is her officers and men who make her a fighting ship. The training, equipment and spirit of the PT crews will make more difference in winning this war than anything the designers and builders of Elco PT's can ever do.

## THE PT'S AIR ARM

_(Continued from page 13)_

As elsewhere, in foxholes 'round the world, we Americans came to know one another better. But not all was fun and laughter in the conversation. Sometimes, before the group had realized it, mention was made of those who had been killed in night landings or shot down by Jap night fighters or anti-aircraft fire, or of those who had died when their fragile PT boats had been caught in cross fire from Jap warships. Gallant fighting men had given their lives that the "Tokio Express" might not run.

When the moon waned, the tempo of activity among the crews increased. The Jap raiders would soon be sweeping down from the north, "down the Slot" between New Georgia and Santa Isabel, into Indispensable Strait, across Sandfly Passage, down into the waters United States forces had to defend. Just after dark each night now, in all but the very worst weather, PT forces and planes were on station, the boats patrolling the top of the channel between Guadalcanal and Tulagi, the SOC's swinging in great circles off Savo Island. Suddenly, close to midnight, a pilot sounds the tally-ho, a signal meaning, "Here they come!" Alert! PT captains answer instantly, pick up speed, move into position. "Six dog-dogs" (destroyers) "approaching at 25 knots, course 090 degrees."

"Two sleepers one mile north." (A second pilot warning that two Jap warships are one mile north of the main column. These may try to flank a PT attack.)

The pilots close in on the warships, give a running commentary on the enemy's formation, speed, course. The motor torpedo boats prepare for action. A seaplane dives at the Japs, raking their decks with machine gun fire. Jap ack-ack snaps back. (The gun flashes will reveal accurately the position of the "Express," thus assisting the PT boats in their stroke.)

The torpedo boats are going in. "Bingo!" from four craft. Tin fish on their way. A moment's wait. A brilliant flash lights the sea. A hit! Bright orange explosions. A Jap destroyer swerves out of column, badly damaged. Jap searchlights snap off and on, seeking the torpedo boats. Flaming tracers lash the air. The 4.7's are cracking. Hard about and away race the little boats, laying smoke. A searchlight picks out a speeding torpedo boat. It twists and turns to escape but the light hangs on. The .50's hammer and the light winks out.

One destroyer remains behind, stern low in the water, her hull erupting in explosion after explosion. A tall, gloomy column of black smoke climbs.

_The opinions or assertions contained herein are the private ones of the writer and are not to be construed as official or reflecting the views of the Navy or the Naval service at large._

## PT—"PLENTY TOUGH"

(Continued from page 25)

rôle. Certainly, there is no need for a boat with living accommodations if the small, fast PT's operate from a base on short sallies after contact has been established by patrol craft and planes. There is also every reason to believe that the PT of the future should be smaller and be stripped down to carry the maximum number of torpedoes at the fastest possible speed.

In recent months, there has been much conjecture as to the development of a PT carrier and certainly no future building program should neglect the careful consideration of such an innovation. As yet, the requirements for ships to carry troops, cargo and ammunition is so great that little experimental work has been carried on in this direction, but the fact that some German armed raiders are reported to have carried motor torpedo boats as supplementary raiding craft shows which way the wind is blowing.

The numerous operations which incorporate the basing, maintaining and repairing of PT boats are a less glamorous but nevertheless essential part of the successful employment of these boats. Without the trained base crews to keep them up to their maximum efficiency, the officers and crews that fight PT's could never have had so high a batting average. Few people realize the long months of training for base personnel and the special equipment required for the proper functioning of these vital groups. From the beginning, the Navy has realized how vital was this service and, as a result, the organization has been patterned after the organization of aviation ground crews. To get a boat back on the firing line in the shortest possible time after casualties and damage have been suffered is the object of all base forces, and the operating personnel of the boats are the first ones to give complete credit to the hard-working base force.

This war has proven that no naval vessel which can keep the sea and carry the ordnance should be neglected in naval building programs in the future, and the history of the PT's in this war demonstrates that they are a proven combat vessel with almost unlimited possibilities of development.

*The opinions or assertions contained herein are the private ones of the writer and are not to be construed as official or reflecting the views of the Navy Department or the Naval service at large.*

## SQUADRON "X"

(Continued from page 7)

Said Chief Torpedoman Marvin Crosson, a quiet, studious boy with a fine knowledge of history, "They're not islands. Guadalcanal is not an island. They're nothing more or less than little points on a map."

"So all right. Let the Japs have 'em."

"That's just it. The Japs did have them, and it was important for us to win them back. Look here." Crosson took a dog-eared map from his pocket and spread it on his knees. "Here we are, right here. North of us the enemy is solid, with a string of stepping stones all the way down from Japan. South are Australia and the sea lanes we must use to defend it. From Guadalcanal the Japs could cover those sea lanes with bombers. See?"

They had known it anyway. Grousing was merely an outlet for cramped emotions. But, when the war was over and the Japs were liquidated, Guadalcanal and Tulagi could turn turtle and sink into the sea, for all these men cared. They wouldn't shed a tear.

A poker game was in progress one afternoon — Ship's Cook Frank O'Malley red hot as always — when the glittering sun was engulfed suddenly by swift clouds that let loose a flood. The men scurried for shelter. When it rained on Tulagi, you took no chances.

They plucked their personal possessions from the floors of huts and tents, hung them on anything handy, and pulled up their feet in the manner of a plane retracting its landing gear. Then dolefully they watched the ground about them turn into a sticky sea of mud. Without the drains they had constructed, Snob Hill would have been a complete washout. Tulagi weather was savage.

The Marines on Guadalcanal knew all about this freakish weather. They had been living and dying in it from the beginning, and their airmen had found it a foe almost as treacherous as the Jap. So did the overworked pilots of a handful of SOC biplanes based on Tulagi.

Brave men flew these Navy planes. They were the eyes of the PT boats, tirelessly searching the seas for signs of enemy activity. The weather made little difference to them. They knew that bad weather was a favorite weapon of the Japs and, under or behind any advancing front of swollen clouds, enemy warships were likely to be on the prowl. Consequently, they went out in the worst of it, under impossible conditions. The day of the poker game, one of them did not come back.

At the base, work went steadily on. In charge of the torpedo shop was Ensign (now Lieutenant jg) Stanley C. Thomas, who could make a torpedo talk. He and Chief Torpedomen Shorty Long and Herbert Wing had little time to be concerned about Tulagi's weather. Sun or rain, they were everlastingly occupied with the boats. It was a six-hour job to get a tin fish ready for firing, and the fish were fired often.

"Ten thousand bucks it costs," said Shorty, "to send one of these babies on its way. We have to be sure they get what they're sent for."

Other men were transferred from boats to base whenever the squadron as a whole had need of their talents. Chief Machinist's Mate Arthur Stuffert left his PT to work in the engine shop. Ship's Cook Charlie May was coaxed against his will to slave in the shore galley. Some of the men liked the change; some didn't. Most of them preferred the boats. Typical was Ship's Cook Lloyd Hummer, who ducked his chores ashore and rode one particular boat at every opportunity, praying for action. "Just lemme at 'em," he begged. "We'll show those apes!"

The man who really ran the base force was Chief Boatswain's Mate Charlie Tufts. Nothing stumped Charlie. No job was too big or too pesky. When tools or parts were needed, he sometimes took a walk — usually to the Marine encampment.

One day, returning from such a stroll, Charlie ambled solemnly into the torpedo shop and began emptying his pockets. A wrench came out. A handful of nuts and bolts. A weird and varied assortment of odds and ends for which the PT men had been tearing their hair. Charlie blinked at his collection. He was a mild man, a little bumpy in places, running short of hair but never of energy or ingenuity. "Now how in the world," he said, "did I ever get all this stuff? My, my. Someone must have framed me."

Those were the lighter interludes. Some of the others were less happily remembered. Like the night of November 7th. Three of the boats were patrolling that night within shouting distance of one another. One was commanded by Lieutenant Hugh M. Robinson, the squadron executive officer. Another was in charge of Lieutenant (jg) James Brent Greene. The third was skippered by Lieutenant (jg) Leonard A. Nikoloric. Youngsters, all of them. Robbie, the oldest, was 27. The other PT skippers had an affectionate name for him. They called him "Poor Old Robbie."

About midnight, the Japs came in. Brent maneuvered for a shot and fired a spread of four torpedoes at the leading enemy ship, a destroyer. One of the fish jammed in its tube. A fountain of sparks leaped skyward and the quiet night was bedlam. Torpedoman Brenton Goddard cleared the tube with a blow of his mallet.

The torpedoes may have winged home or may not. No one was sure. At any rate, the Jap was still in action and the dazzling fireworks of the "hot run" had given him a point of aim for his searchlights. In a heart beat of time, Robbie and Brent were trapped in the lights while the Jap's guns roared their defiance. The enemy was on his toes that night, performing at peak efficiency. His shooting was good. Too good. A salvo of 4.7's screamed from his main battery and one of them exploded with an earthquake roar on Robbie's bow.

Happily, every man on the mosquito boat was at his battle station. All were tossed about like tenpins but none was forward when the shell struck and none was seriously hurt. Where the bow of the boat had been, however, was now only a jagged mass of plywood splinters. The PT opened fire with her .50 caliber machine guns and struggled to escape.

"We in our boat," Lieutenant Nikoloric recalls, "heard the explosion just after getting in a shot. We saw what happened. Robbie's boat was less than 100 yards abeam of us, and the glare of the shell burst lit up the night all around us. We thought it was all over for Robbie and his gang. If that shell hadn't finished them, the next hit certainly would. The Japs were sending everything they had at her."

Owen Pearle, Nick's radioman, sent out a yell over the radio to find out who was alive over there. Someone was, because Robbie's machine guns were crackling. But, after what had happened, there had to be casualties. "Are you okay?" Pearle begged. "Are you all right?"

It was Lieutenant Robinson himself who answered. "Hell, yes!" he barked. "We're heading for home!" Despite the loss of her bow, the crippled boat was running with all the speed she could manage, executing a series of wobbly maneuvers that kept the enemy's shells wide of the mark. Meanwhile, Gunner's Mate Ben Parrish, wedged in his turret, clung fast to the grips of his guns and coolly shot out the destroyer's searchlights. It was sweet shooting.

The boat churned on, throwing up fountains of spray. She was getting away. But the Japs had a perfect target. The smoke generator had jammed, and the Jap had the range. Chief Torpedoman Alfred Norwood, an oldtimer with what was needed, started for the smoke pot. Soaking wet, half blinded, barely able to keep his feet on the twisting deck, he fell on the generator and tore at it with his hands. It had to work. Without smoke, the PT was doomed. There, on his knees, Norwood wrestled with the valves while enemy shells crackled overhead like whips.

The valves let go and smoke gushed out — but backward. Now the smoke used on the motor torpedo boats is a chemical mixture shot forth under pressure. It is thick and strangling. It burns cruelly, like acid, and can sear the skin off a man's face or hands quickly. Norwood was caught in the hissing stream and stumbled back out of it, his face and arms in torment. But he went back in. He got his hands on the balky generator and stayed there, pounding it, until the smoke poured out the way it was supposed to. In all this time, the enemy's fire had not diminished.

With the white screen swelling in her wake, the PT at last shook off pursuit and left the Jap astern. Then Norwood looked at his hands. They were bright red, covered with thin, bulging blisters that broke and peeled away. They were aflame to the elbows. Norwood walked forward on the heaving deck and sat down by the port turret and was sick. But, without question, his coolness and ability in a grave emergency had saved the lives of his shipmates.

It was that way often in the little thunder boats. Fate put the finger on some one man and challenged him: "Brother, it's your turn." The chosen individual might be the skipper, the second in command, a man at the guns or a machinist's mate in the engine room. Officers or enlisted men, it made no difference. Fate played no favorites. Suddenly for a brief, bright flash of time, the lives of all aboard would depend on one man's ability and courage. None knew when his turn might come.

The PT made port that night, limping through the dark with the sea growling in her vitals. It was incredible, but it happened. The Jap who had crippled her was less lucky. Too avid for the kill, he forgot the other PT and left himself unprotected. His searchlight beams and the bright light of his gunbursts were a tempting target. The PT, with Nick at the wheel, Lieutenant (jg) Bernie O'Neill and Chief Quartermaster John Legg spotting, had stalked him half way across the Slot. Now she slipped up on his silent side, away from the thunder of the guns, and loosed her torpedoes.

A few hours later, Chief Yeoman John Wicks stood on an upturned box in front of the squadron office and, with red and white paint dripping brightly from his brush, added yet another Jap flag to the PT emblem over the doorway.

The Guadalcanal Marines were sleeping better. The Japs were learning, the hard way, that Sleepless Lagoon was an area of peril, patrolled by savage little thunder bugs whose sting was often fatal.

## WHERE THEY LEARN TO BE TOUGH

*(Continued from page 29)*

value to new squadrons undergoing training. They are naturally made as realistic as possible, in view of the fact that following their shakedown periods the new squadrons are immediately sent to their assigned areas in the various theaters of operation. Very frequently, additional training is obtained in southern waters en route to the actual combat zones. This period varies in duration for the different squadrons in accordance with the prearranged plans for shipment of the boats. Not only is this strenuous training of great benefit to the officers and men, but it also seems to show up certain material casualties in the boats, which are thereafter corrected in the short post-shakedown operations which these boats have been given before leaving the mainland.

"One of the outstanding characteristics of officers involved in the PT program is their constant and unending efforts and thoughts to improve in every manner possible the effectiveness and battle efficiency of our MTBs. In other words, this is basically a young man's job and, with the typical attitude of young Americans not to become complacent or satisfied with a *status quo* condition, there is an abundance of ideas and thoughts constantly being submitted and mulled over to achieve exactly the foregoing results."

There are numerous secondary PT schools which supplement the instruction given at Melville and among the most interesting of these are those at Miami and at the Naval Division of The Electric Boat Company at Bayonne, N. J.

All is not fighting aboard these "weapons of opportunity." There are, unfortunately, times when the PT's are forced to limp into some obscure cove in the hope of repairing combat damage. For this reason, it is essential that officers and crew members of the advance base units have a specific knowledge of the construction of their craft so that they can make repairs with the tools and spare parts which are available. The first PT Repair and Maintenance School was established at the Elco Plant in the autumn of 1940 by Lieut. Commander Walter Rowe, who is the Navy's Assistant Supervisor of Shipbuilding at Bayonne. At that time, the M.T.B.S.T.C. at Melville did not exist, with the result that for nearly two years Elco's "Naval Academy," as it is affectionately referred to by its students, was the Navy's only specialized PT training school.

During a course ranging from two to six weeks, both officers and crew members not only study blueprints in their classrooms but also follow every step of construction in the Elco plant. Here they are assisted by expert carpenters, joiners, electricians, plumbers, boatbuilders and other specialists. Instructive motion pictures are provided, lectures are given on specific subjects and particular attention is paid to engine intricacies and installation. Not the least important of the school's curriculum are occasional visits to the nearby Brooklyn Navy Yard where the fitting out of PT squadrons is constantly going on.

Attached to the famous Subchaser Training Center at Miami is a PT shakedown detail, which is conducted by Commander Alan R. Montgomery (who established it in April, 1943) and a staff of five young officers. Here they are not interested in academic theories of PT boat operation but deal in actual experience and actual problems. At Miami, they practice with live bullets and live torpedoes and when a PT crew is pronounced fit for combat duty, it has experienced about every situation it will have to face except perhaps the actual peril of enemy gunfire.

PT boats, although they pack a lethal wallop in the shape of depth charges, are not primarily designed for anti-submarine warfare. The PT boat is perfectly willing to leave the task of sinking submarines to her bigger sisters. She has another job to do, a job peculiarly her own, which she has done with astonishing success; she hunts for bigger game. Commander Montgomery defines a PT craft as follows: "A fast, small boat, carrying a heavy armament of torpedoes used principally under cover of darkness to torpedo large enemy ships."

In these laconic words, spoken with the Navy's love of brevity, lie the secret and the triumph of these tiny craft. "Under cover of darkness" means that the PT boat strikes at night. "Large enemy ships" means not only freighters and transports but destroyers and cruisers and battleships. No ship is too big for a PT boat to tackle, as the Japanese have found out to their sorrow. "The bigger, the better," is the PT's fighting slogan.

Commander Montgomery's own record is to a large extent a saga of the PT boat, proof that "the bigger they are, the harder they fall." Montgomery, as a lieutenant commander, headed the first squadron of PT boats assigned to the Guadalcanal sector. The squadron went into action in October, 1942. Montgomery was invalided home in November, the following month, but his famous "Squadron X," continuing operations under the leadership of Lieut. Hugh M. Robinson, went on to pile up a "bag" which included a Jap cruiser, six destroyers and a patrol ship.

Commander Montgomery's hard-bitten shakedown school, as has been emphasized before, is not concerned with textbook theories of motor torpedo boat warfare. "We give them the cold facts here, the real thing," he says. "The course of instruction at the shakedown school is a brief, intensive period of operational instruction. The crews are put through tactics, gunnery, torpedo firing, aircraft defense, night training and maneuvers. Most of the training is done at night because that is when the PT boat is active. No crews are released as fit for combat duty until they have become proficient enough to go instantly into battle."

While the problem of training crews is the most vital task of the shakedown school, it is also concerned with eliminating "bugs" from the boats and in seeking constantly to improve the craft and the scope and effectiveness of the equipment they carry. Despite the tremendous strain that the PT's are subjected to in the course of operations in all types of weather, they rarely quit. "I think it something the builders of these boats should be proud of," declared Montgomery. "Whenever the call goes out for a squadron to go out for practice, rarely is a boat unable to comply."

Commander Montgomery is 38, the oldest officer at the school. His staff consists of five officers who average about 24 years of age. Four of them were in Montgomery's famous Guadalcanal squadron: Lieut. Robert Searles, of Leonia, N. J.; Lieut. R. C. Wark, of Pasadena, Calif.; Lieut. Leonard Nikoloric, of Englewood, N. J.; and Ensign Charles Tufts, of Batesville, Ind. The fifth member of the shakedown staff is Ensign J. M. Flackmann, of St. Louis, Mo. All PT boats are equipped with two-way voice radios and the Commander and his staff keep in constant touch with the PT's as they engage in practice far out at sea. Oftentimes the "Skipper" goes along; he likes nothing better than to nurse a recalcitrant motor to all out performance or to feel the throb of powerful engines under his hands again.

One thing is certain about PT duty; once a man gets into it, he rarely asks for a transfer to another branch of the Navy. Montgomery and his staff believe the answer is simple. PT duty is popular with seamen because of its informality, its freedom from the duties and strictures in a bigger ship. It is attractive to young officers because it is the quickest way to get a command. PT boats may be commanded by officers with the rank of ensign or lieutenant, jg. The only comparable command is that of a plane.

The real attraction of PT duty probably lies even deeper than this: in the opportunity to rise above the level of the crowd, to exercise initiative and individuality in judgment and work, in the thrill and excitement of actual combat with the enemy at almost insuperable odds. David must have had the same thrill when he opened up on Goliath with his sling. The PT boat is no fad and will remain as an integral part of the Navy after the war, Montgomery believes. "The value of motor torpedo boats in warfare cannot be overestimated. Here is a tiny craft, costing around a quarter of a million dollars, manned by only eleven men and yet capable of sinking a battleship costing a hundred million dollars. The PT boat has only one rival when cost, speed and deadly effectiveness are considered: the airplane. There is one vital difference between the two, however. The plane does its most effective work against naval units in daylight hours; the PT boat strikes at night."

"We are constantly improving the speed, accuracy and striking power of the PT boats. All of our craft are subjected to the most rigorous tests possible; actual battle conditions are simulated to the last detail. As soon as a defect is uncovered, the fact is communicated to the builder through official channels. Thus, when the new boats roll off the line, the improvements are incorporated in them. We get as nearly perfect boats as technical knowledge and constant, gruelling battle tests can evolve."

As for the future, Montgomery reminds us that PT boats are primarily a weapon of opportunity. "As this war progresses, there will be many opportunities for them to be used. The battle of Guadalcanal provided an ideal setup. Guadalcanal, at the start of the engagement, was too hot a place for big warships to remain. They could come in and strike but would have to retire. PT boats, by their ability to prowl at night and hide out by day up jungle streams and amid mangrove bushes, were admirably suited for this type of warfare. Opportunities similar to that at Guadalcanal will undoubtedly present themselves in the task of driving the Japs back to Tokyo. The Japs have a lot of ships yet to be sunk and the PT boats undoubtedly will get their share."

## THE PT'S BOX SCORE

(Continued from page 9)

Four PT's then on patrol attacked at 500 yards and scored two torpedo hits on an enemy cruiser, after which the bombardment ceased and the Japanese retired. The PT's were then pursued by Japanese destroyers but suffered no losses, and in turn inflicted damage on the Jap destroyers' bridges with .50 caliber fire. There is a strong possibility that a cruiser seen to sink the next day was the one hit by the PT's.

On the 29th of October, two Japanese destroyers were reported to be in the vicinity. Two PT's patrolling near Savo Island intercepted one of the destroyers and made one sure torpedo hit which resulted in her sinking. On November 8th, 1942, aircraft reconnaissance revealed that five destroyers were heading down toward Esperance from the northwest. Three boats patrolling between Savo and Esperance sighted the destroyers close aboard, heading south at about 30 knots. The PT's attacked at a range of about 1000 yards and made one sure torpedo hit but they were caught in a heavy three-way crossfire and one PT had her bow shot away. Despite this, the damaged PT was able to make port under her own power and the motor torpedo boat tender at the base improvised a new plywood bow. This particular boat was soon in action again. It was later reported that the torpedo hit made in this engagement caused the Jap to blow up.

On November 10th, three PT's were patrolling southwest of Savo when they sighted four destroyers in column close to the shore. Contact was then lost against the dark background. The PT's, headed in the direction that the destroyers were last observed to be steaming, were suddenly illuminated and fired upon by the enemy. This forced the PT's to fire their torpedoes at 1000 yards' range. One torpedo hit was claimed. On November 13th, five PT's were on their way to a rendezvous off Savo Island when enemy destroyers were sighted. In all, eight torpedoes were fired at rather long range. Results were not observed since the boats were recalled immediately and ordered to intercept Japanese ships coming in to shell Henderson Field. The PT's did so and, at a range of 1200 yards, one PT fired three torpedoes at a large warship and one hit was observed. Another PT fired two torpedoes at a destroyer and made one hit. The most important result was that the Japanese were forced to cease shelling and retired.

On December 7th, four PT's which were standing an alert patrol sighted five destroyers screening a large ship. The PT's fired in all 14 torpedoes, making two sure hits and two additional probable hits. The Japanese forces were dispersed and contact was lost. On December 9th, two PT's on patrol near Kamimbo Bay sighted a submarine on the surface. As the boats turned to attack, the submarine submerged and, as she did, the PT's picked up a Japanese landing boat close aboard. They opened fire on the landing boat with machine guns and 20 mm. While this was going on, one of them observed the submarine to surface. Two torpedoes were fired, one making a direct hit amidships which completely destroyed the undersea raider. On December 11th, eight Japanese destroyers were sighted by patrolling torpedo boats. In the surprise attack that followed, torpedo hits were scored on three of the destroyers, and one Jap was hit and left burning and buckling amidships.

On January 11th, 1943, PT's on patrol sighted a force of seven destroyers coming in to land troops and supplies. In the stiffly contested engagement that followed, the Japanese lost one destroyer and another was severely damaged by torpedo hits. The torpedo boats were destroyed in this engagement, one by fire and one by beaching, but many of the crew were saved. The following morning the PT's destroyed great quantities of stores and supplies which the Japanese destroyers had tried to float into the beach of the northwest tip of Guadalcanal. On January 14th and 15th, 1943, 13 PT's tangled with seven Jap warships. The results of this action were a hit by torpedoes on one enemy light cruiser and one enemy destroyer. On January 28th, the Japanese attempted to land stores by sending de-

stroyers in near shore at high speed to drop supplies, hoping that they would float ashore. The PT's drove the destroyers away and, with the aid of our planes, destroyed the supplies by machine gun fire. On February 11th, PT's engaged an enemy force of 20 destroyers near Guadalcanal. At least one destroyer was sunk, two others were torpedoed and believed to have been sunk, and the entire force was turned away. Our losses were three PT boats.

During the time that the squadrons and boats comprising Flotilla One were so active around the Solomons, other boats attached to the New Guinea area command patrolled nightly in the Huon Gulf and participated in many engagements against enemy destroyers and larger warships. On December 24th, 1942, at Douglas Harbor (Papua), two PT's on patrol sighted two Japanese landing craft heading out of the mouth of Douglas Harbor. A machine gun battle ensued for about ten minutes, during which time both Japanese barges were sunk. On January 17th, 1943, in the same locality, one PT sighted three landing barges and attacked, being opposed by 20 mm. and light machine gun fire. The engagement lasted about 25 minutes, when two of the landing craft had been sunk and the third was on fire.

Other engagements with landing craft in the same area around Douglas Bay (Papua) totaled 17 landing craft sunk as well as three more badly damaged. Through all these actions, despite the fact that the PT's were usually outnumbered about three to one, they suffered only negligible damage. These actions can best be described as melees, resulting from the fact that immediate attacks must be made without conforming to prearranged plans. Also encountered by PT's operating in the New Guinea area was a large damaged Jap ship of between 6000 and 8000 tons, which was torpedoed and sunk. Still later, a large submarine, discharging supplies for the encircled Japanese troops near Buna, was sunk.

In addition to the above mentioned actions there were many additional engagements and near-engagements. These served an important, if less positive, function of keeping the enemy away from the shores and of furnishing a harassing influence which was a large factor in hampering Japanese operations. A steady stream of PT boats is now en route to various areas in the Pacific. Since the arrival of the first squadrons at Tulagi, on October 13th, 1942, many new boats of a later design have arrived, with many others on the way. Thus the previously insignificant stepchildren of our Navy are gradually winning their rightful recognition as a necessary and important arm of our service. When the final pages on history of naval sea power in the Pacific are written, it is certain that our motor torpedo boats will have contributed their proportionate share.

Thus far, the PT squadrons in the Solomons have sunk or damaged an estimated 300,000 tons of enemy vessels, including a battleship or heavy cruiser, two cruisers, sixteen destroyers and one submarine with a loss of only a relatively small number of boats, of which some of the crews were saved.

PT personnel are especially proud of a despatch which they received from Admiral Halsey, in which he complimented the Tulagi-based boats, extending sincere congratulations to the entire personnel upon their gallant and successful operations, despite the extremely dangerous proximity of enemy forces. He went on to commend them for their many attacks on the "Tokyo Express," the success of which relieved much of the pressure imposed on our hard-pressed South Pacific forces. He wished them continued success against the enemy — told them to keep hitting 'em!

*The opinions or assertions contained herein are not to be construed as official or reflecting the views of the Navy or the Naval service at large.*

*Illustrating her famed agility, an Elco PT banks sharply on a fast turn.*

# *Elco* **PTs**

## THE INSIDE STORY OF THE PTs

(Continued from page 33)

the three planes were smoking and losing altitude rapidly. The probability is that they never got back to their base.

For gallantry displayed in the action, both officers and men were cited by General MacArthur.

### Enemy Ship Fired at Her Dock

The PTs left destruction in their wake wherever enemy craft were found. In most cases vessels that fell prey to PT torpedoes were caught either at sea or at their base. On the Philippine coast one night Lieut. Bulkeley and Ensign Anthony Akers found a Japanese ship moored at the dock. They fired two torpedoes at this vessel. One torpedo found its mark and set the vessel afire. The next morning it was reported that an enemy tanker was still burning alongside her dock. Again the PT had struck home. All craft are fair game for the motor torpedo boats. Probably this vessel was completely lost.

### Ruse Traps Japanese on Beach

Though practically all of the PTs' offensive operations were confined to patrols and raids by night, a party would occasionally be organized to cruise along the Bataan shore, a ruse designed to draw the enemy's fire and thus reveal the positions of his gun emplacements.

On one of these occasions as the PTs cruised along the beach, not more than three or four hundred yards offshore, troops came down to the beach and gazed in consternation. Perhaps they wanted a first-hand view of what had been described to them in a Tokio radio broadcast as a "monster with flapping wings which makes a lot of noise and fires torpedoes in all directions!"

At any rate this time the mythical bird-boat opened up with .50-caliber guns and raked the beach, killing eight enemy troops and wounding fourteen.

Lieutenants Bulkeley and Kelly were an inseparable pair that often worked as a team in their various operations. One trick they tried was to put Kelly in ambush at the north end of Subic Bay while Bulkeley circled about at high speed in the center of the bay, firing volleys to simulate conditions of an attack. The idea was to draw enemy ships out in pursuit in order to give Kelly a chance to close in and drive home a torpedo. By this time, however, the Japs were wary and refused to be drawn out.

### Hundreds Saved in Manila Evacuation

As Manila was about to fall, all available craft were pressed into the service of evacuating the citizen inhabitants. Among these vessels was the S.S. Corregidor, a transport with a capacity of 1200 persons.

Bound out through the difficult mined channels past Corregidor Island, she was sunk. It was night and the only craft that came to her assistance was a group of PT boats. Skimming back and forth over the hidden mine fields where sudden death and destruction lurked at a depth of only a few feet, three of Lieut. Bulkeley's boats went to the rescue.

Loaded to capacity, the PTs saved 282 persons. Were it not for their light draft and great carrying capacity, this part of the saga of PT exploits in action could never have been written. Lieut. Bulkeley's boat alone picked up 196 survivors in addition to her crew and carried them all safely to Corregidor in one trip.

### MacArthur's Judgment Vindicated

All the world respects General Douglas MacArthur as a man of magnificent courage, inspiring leadership, rare judgment and imagination. Interwoven in the tale of his epic defense of the Philippines and his subsequent transfer to Australia where he was ordered by his Commander-in-Chief to assume supreme command, is the story of the vindication of his faith in the motor torpedo boat as a mighty weapon of modern warfare — an important cog in the machinery of total warfare.

When orders came from President Roosevelt to break through the Japanese blockade of Luzon and proceed to Australia, a crucial question arose: How to go? It would be a hazardous venture at best, involving extreme danger by any route. All of the plans for an Allied offensive in the southwest Pacific may be said to have hinged on his decision.

Plane or submarine was the suggestion of those whose advice was based on traditional conceptions. But General MacArthur never was tradition-bound. Conferring with Lieut. Bulkeley, who shared his enthusiasm for the motor torpedo boat as a "weapon of opportunity," he seized this opportunity to demonstrate that the strategy borne of tradition-defying imagination is the strategy carrying the greatest odds for success.

Each Elco PT carries four of these .50-caliber anti-aircraft machine guns in twin turrets

It was a momentous decision. On the PT he staked his chance of getting through to his new post, on it the safety of his wife and son, the lives of his staff . . . and his own. Almost without exception his venture was branded desperate — by some, even fantastic.

Under such circumstances it was that he sent this reply to his Commander-in-Chief:

"We go with the fall of the moon;
We go during the Ides of March."

And thus it was that, in the gathering dusk of the evening of March 11, a midget armada of four Elco motor torpedo boats, carrying the General's party of twenty-one, slipped through the almost air-tight blockade of Corregidor. MacArthur found the single leak.

Jap warships constituted a formidable blockade indeed. Hostile guns studded the shores. Enemy planes maintained ceaseless patrol. Submarines lurked in dangerous waters.

Stifling a desire, no doubt, to ram a torpedo through one of the Jap warships just for good luck, Lieut. Bulkeley led the speeding squadron out into the open sea, eluding surface craft, skimming over hidden mine fields. Swinging south, he laid a course down the island coast, while flashing lights ashore revealed that the roar of a dozen Packards had been mistaken by the enemy for the approach of Allied planes.

Smashing through 20-foot seas, the four boats sped southward through the night, fanning out on divergent courses before daybreak to rendezvous at dawn by pre-arranged plan in the jungle-fringed cove of a tropical island.

Machine guns were trained on MacArthur's craft as she headed for the entrance to the cove — but they were friendly guns. One PT of the little flotilla had already arrived and they were cleared for action in case the approaching boat should prove hostile.

Here a submarine was available to take the General and his party if he chose, but again it was decided that the torpedo boats offered the best chance of success. Lying over in the secluded harbor during daylight hours, the party set out once more as night fell — this time in three boats.

That evening Japanese destroyers appeared on the horizon, but the nearly invisible PTs merely stopped, escaping detection. Crossing in the wake of the enemy ships, they resumed the southerly course, at dawn slipping again into another remote island harbor where bombers were to pick the party up for the flight to Australia.

Three days later the planes arrived, to find the motor torpedo boats awaiting them. The PTs had successfully played their part in running a hazardous gantlet and once again had aided General MacArthur in outwitting the enemy.

### Based on Cebu

His task of evacuating General MacArthur from the Philippines successfully accomplished, Lieut. Bulkeley was ordered back to a base on the island of Cebu, 375 miles to the southeastward of Bataan. Again the PTs were destined to find themselves in the thick of combat.

Here, for the first time in three months, the battle-tested (but seldom battle-scarred) boats found facilities which would permit hauling out and a measure of the servicing for which they were long overdue.

Behind that simple statement lies a story as dramatic as that of any of their brilliant achievements in action. No tribute is too high to pay to the skill, the ingenuity, the downright determination that alone enabled Lieut. Bulkeley and his men to keep that little group of PTs going — come hell or high water.

Official U. S. Navy Photograph

*Backlighted against a glittering southern sea this Elco PT boat, greeting a task force returning to Hawaii, furnished an official U. S. Navy photographer a chance to make this remarkable shot of a mosquito boat. The mosquito boat was cruising off Pearl Harbor when the task force returned*

Imagine these war boats on their ceaseless vigil, patrolling in the dead of night, under all kinds of weather conditions, going to sea when waves ran 20 feet high, running blacked-out through débris-littered waters, skirting dangerous coasts in darkness without benefit of charts or navigational aids to guide them!

There were no shipyards or drydocks for the PTs. If they happened to smash into a submerged obstruction at night and bend a shaft or damage a strut, they might beach the boat with the tide to repair it themselves if opportunity offered. Or they might have a native diver go down to effect such repairs as he could without beaching. In this manner bent wheels were straightened, shafts trued and struts changed.

There were no facilities, no supplies, no spare parts to draw upon. Servicing, under conditions as Lieut. Bulkeley found them, meant that his officers and men had to turn to and repair what equipment they had as best they could. The finest testimonial to how good that best was is indelibly written in the record showing that these boats were kept running until their mission was completed.

And, indeed, it is no small tribute to the stamina and dependability wrought into these craft by their Bayonne builders that, under such conditions, they could stand the gaff . . . and deliver the goods.

Bulkeley's men turned plumbers, electricians, painters, boatbuilders, machinists, technicians of every description — as the necessity arose. Perhaps that gives a clue as to why the cream of Navy personnel is picked to man the PTs. One brief story illustrates well the indomitable spirit that fired these men. One night on patrol, a PT hit a submerged log. Immediately they beached her — a craft that normally should have a special steel cradle and crane to take her out of the water. Ashore, they stripped her armament and other equipment, then travelled afoot sixty miles south along the island. Returning later, they salvaged that PT, patched her up and got her back in commission.

If that isn't resourcefulness, invincibility, then such traits don't exist. Nothing could stop these PT crews.

Yet Lieut. Bulkeley, questioned as to feats of this kind, gives all credit to his officers, his men, his boats, and says: "We have done nothing more than our duty. We have done only what is expected of us — no more, no less."

### Quezons Evacuated to Mindanao

One of Lieut. Bulkeley's assignments was to aid in the evacuation of Manuel Quezon, President of the Commonwealth of the Philippines. Holding on at Corregidor until departure was imperative, Quezon's presence in the islands had stiffened resistance there and inspired the Filipinos in their last-ditch fight side by side with American troops.

The tactics used to get President Quezon, his wife, two daughters and son, Sergio Osmena his Vice-President, and other members of his Cabinet out of the Philippines were the same as those which had crowned General MacArthur's venture with success two weeks earlier. This time, however, Quezon's party left Corregidor by submarine which took them to Negros, an island to the southward below Paney.

When seven Japanese destroyers surrounded the immediate point where Quezon was believed to be, it became imperative to make an effort to evacuate the President to avoid his capture by the enemy. Lieut. Bulkeley had no choice as to time when the moon wasn't out, and with aerial reconnaissance showing seven Japanese destroyers in the immediate vicinity, he ran past the destroyers, picked the President and his party up and returned to Mindanao where the President was evacuated by bombers.

No small part was played in this episode by Lieut. Bulkeley. President Quezon had received a radio message from Lieut. Gen. Wainright directing him to remain on the island due to the heavy concentration of hostile ships around the island. President Quezon took one look at Lieut. Bulkeley's beard and black cigar and his person dressed in heavy rain clothes with a southwester atop his head. Said he, "This man is a Spanish pirate, a sea wolf of the old days. He can take me out. I go with you." With 120 miles to go and heavy seas breaking over the craft all the way, the PT boat never faltered and landed its precious cargo safely ashore.

### Cruiser Sunk at Cebu

A 6,000-ton light cruiser of the Kuma class was next to find PT torpedoes just as deadly as those of a destroyer.

On Cebu is located the second largest city in the Philippines, second only to Manila. Allied forces at the time were being withdrawn from Bataan to Corregidor and the enemy was massing power at Cebu to effect a landing on that island.

A force of 12,000 troops aboard ten transports protected by five warships was involved in the landing operations, strongly supported by tanks, dive-bombers, and a heavy naval barrage laid down by the warships.

Three o'clock one afternoon word came through from Army spotters on the beach that a Japanese cruiser, accompanied by destroyers, was seen heading for the southern tip of Cebu, 75 miles from where the PTs were based. Lieut. Bulkeley laid his plans for a midnight attack in the narrow strait that separates Cebu from Negros.

Ensign Cox as usual was running Lieut. Bulkeley's flagship, PT-41, and Lieut. Kelly had Ensign Richardson with him aboard PT-34. Together they slipped down the coast and a half-hour before midnight were ready to attack.

As the cruiser appeared around the point, guarded by a destroyer in her wake and three others outside of her, Bulkeley and Kelly went into action — the odds a hundred to one against them, on a tonnage basis. The PTs could have been swung on their adversary's davits like dinghies aboard a yacht.

Charging down directly on the cruiser's course so that only her forward guns could be brought to bear, Bulkeley swerved off to starboard and then, with one of those maneuvers that only a PT could execute at such speed, went into a sharp turn on a collision course for the cruiser's port side.

Two torpedoes launched at point-blank range went home, one exploding under the bridge. Strafing the ship to draw enemy fire, Bulkeley paved the way for Kelly, just astern. As Bulkeley sheered off to go astern of the cruiser he found himself pocketed between her and the destroyer . . . with three other destroyers ahead — hitherto unseen!

© M. Rosenfeld

*A view of an Elco PT at speed that is enjoyed by all aviators of the United Nations only*

Kelly in the meantime had his hands full with heavy shell fire from six-inch guns and strong searchlight illumination. Duplicating Bulkeley's maneuver, he closed in to 300 yards and fired two torpedoes. At that range, hits were inevitable. As a shell from the cruiser swept away the mast over Kelly's head, his torpedoes crashed into the ship's magazine. A deafening explosion followed and, engulfed in smoke, the cruiser went down by the stern, sinking completely in twenty minutes.

Breaking into a U-turn that swept him back toward the cruiser's course northward, Kelly gave his PT-34 the gun, with a destroyer in hot pursuit. During the course of a 30-mile chase up the coast of Cebu, the destroyer hurled 23 salvos from her six-inch guns, without scoring a single hit.

Bulkeley, with two destroyers out to get him, dodged five salvos and lost the enemy on a long chase to Mindanao. Speed, and maneuverability, had saved his life. Perhaps that's why, today, he is so insistent in his demand for speed — more speed — at all costs.

## Kelly Gets a Dive Bomber

At any range, the Japs had found the PTs harder to hit than an atom, their only target a cloud of flying spray skipping wavetops at a mile a minute.

In a quick maneuver, Kelly lost the destroyer that was chasing him. Forty miles he navigated up the coast in darkness, with little but instinct to guide him. When, by his reckoning, he calculated that he should be off the entrance to Cebu Harbor, he could not risk the hazardous channel with neither charts nor lights to guide him in.

The only alternative was to wait for dawn. But dawn brought with it enemy planes starting their morning patrol. Just as he got into the narrow entrance to the channel, four dive-bombers spotted him and dove to attack. Bombs were being released at 300 feet. Swooping down to 100, the warplanes strafed the PT in desperate attack.

With no sea room to equalize the odds against him, Kelly zigzagged up the tortuous channel. Three of his guns were shot away, they manned the fourth to the end, and with it accounted for one of the four bombers just before making an escape by running PT-34 up on the beach.

The shell that sheared off Kelly's mast in the cruiser attack was the nearest approximation to a direct hit the Japs could claim in all these actions in the islands. While a fragment from one of the bombs in the dive-bombing attack did pierce their hull, it can also be said that not one of the PT squadron was lost as a direct result of enemy fire.

Their mission accomplished, Lieutenants Bulkeley and Kelly, with Ensigns Akers and Cox, were flown out of the Philippines to Australia and then back to the United States to the welcome which they so richly deserve.

Considering the results Lieutenant Bulkeley achieved as commander of only a handful of PTs, it is not too difficult to picture the possibilities if he had a hundred at his disposal.

America salutes her PT heroes!

## PTs at Pearl Harbor

While the Philippines were the central theatre of action for the motor torpedo boats thus far in the battle of the Pacific, they had already distinguished themselves at the very outbreak of war during the attack on Pearl Harbor on December 7.

At the time that the raiding Japanese planes appeared over Hawaii, four Elco PTs were loaded on the deck of a fleet tanker for shipment. Ensign Arthur H. Bryant of Alexandria, Virginia, and three other young ensigns, commanding the four boats, were aboard and ready to sail when the first waves of enemy bombers began to darken the skies.

In the rain of explosives that followed, the ensigns instantly ordered their gun crews into action, bringing down at least one of the enemy planes. A second plane was reported as probably destroyed.

Subsequent advices reveal that other PTs were afloat at the time and in action. One report mentions that an enemy submarine operating outside the harbor was spotted by American fliers, who dropped smoke bombs to indicate the submarine's position. The PTs circled the area and laid down a pattern of depth charges, which are believed to have destroyed the sub.

A number of midget two-man submarines were also operating in and about the harbor during the attack, and one of these is also reliably reported to have been sunk in a brush with the torpedo boats.

## Action in Other Theatres

When the history of the present world war is written, some of its most stirring chapters will inevitably recount the dramatic engagements in which motor torpedo boats played a leading role during the years prior to America's entry into the conflict.

In them, the exploits of Elco-built PTs will find a prominent place just as their ML's and sub-chasers did when the submarine menace was challenged and overcome a quarter-century ago. Elco PTs have been in constant service across the Atlantic with British forces during the early war years. Details at present are often lacking, but a round-up of all available reports would indicate that they are distinguishing themselves in the European conflict as they have in the Philippines.

Limitations of space forbid a detailed account of what is already known today. But our story of their accomplishments would hardly be complete without brief reference, at least, to some of the highlights.

## With the Commandos at St. Nazaire

In one of the most spectacular combined land-water operations since the historic raid on Zeebrugge in World War I, Commandos cooperated with

*M. Rosenfeld*

*The 20 m.m. cannon shown at the stern is the latest innovation added to the Elco PTs for the edification of all pirates*

British air and naval forces in an assault on the German-held submarine base at St. Nazaire on the French invasion coast.

The drydock at St. Nazaire was the only one on the Atlantic coast of France that could hold an Axis battleship of the Tirpitz class. Furthermore, its destruction would tie up Nazi U-boat activities at this port for at least a year.

Late in March of this Spring, H.M.S. Campbeltown (the former U. S. destroyer Buchanan) was loaded with five tons of delayed action high explosives. After a night crossing of the Channel, she reached her objective and ran up into the approach channel to meet a storm of shell-fire, in the play of searchlights from ship and shore. Observers said the fighting raged at ranges as close as 50 yards.

Smashing her way through obstructions guarding the entrance to the lock, the destroyer was rammed through the center of the main lock gate at 20 knots, plunging half-way through.

Commandos stormed ashore on their job of demolition. As they blasted harbor installations, power houses, pumping stations, dock operating gear, bridges and buildings, the delayed action charges tore the old Campbeltown asunder in a terrific explosion, demolishing the gate and blocking the entrance with her shattered wreckage.

Into this inferno, a motor torpedo boat had followed the destroyer, standing by to torpedo the gate in case the Campbeltown should fail to get through. When motor launches had gotten the destroyer's crew ashore, the PT fired two delayed action torpedoes into the old entrance gate beside the main gate.

Later it was learned that German naval officers had demanded that two of the British officers go aboard the Campbeltown with them as a guarantee that no explosives would be found aboard. Immediately the British officers acquiesced and, just as the party of officers and engineers were making their tour of inspection, the destroyer blew up.

A day elapsed before some semblance of order could be restored from the chaos and confusion that reigned after the raid. That evening, when everything was presumably under control, the PT's torpedoes, fired the night before, blew up and annihilated the old lock entrance.

Renewed fighting immediately broke out between the Nazis and native French, who fought at the side of the Commandos. It was days before a measure of calm prevailed once more at the Nazi-held port. But Allied flags will fly where swastikas wave today before Nazi subs are docked again at St. Nazaire.

## MTBs Score Hits on Prinz Eugen

Heavy weather, which was said at the time to be entirely unsuited to their operation, failed to stop British motor torpedo boats from joining in the action in mid-February when a German fleet, led by the 26,000-ton battleships Scharnhorst and Gneisenau and the 10,000-ton Prinz Eugen, ran the Channel blockade from Brest in Nazi-occupied France to the German naval base at Kiel.

Escorted by 300 planes, the enemy fleet was about to enter the Straits of Dover when all available MTBs (motor torpedo boats) in the Dover area were ordered to sea to join in the action. Heavy seas were running, yet the torpedo boats, according to Admiralty communiqués, put to sea at full speed.

The main units of the enemy fleet were screened by destroyers and German E-boats — a torpedo boat type larger and slower than the British MTB. Though visibility was bad, heavy shore batteries on both sides of the Channel opened up. Dive-bombers screaming overhead swooped low and strafed the attackers with machine gun and cannon fire, while the enemy ships opened up with heavier guns.

In the teeth of this barrage, the MTBs closed in and made their attack.

*M. Rosenfeld*

*Elco 57 Motor Yachts. These Elco 57 Motor Yachts formerly made for pleasure cruising. Many of them, however, are now in service with the Coast Guard for coastal patrol. They are armed with depth charges. Twin Screw boats of this type are most suitable for service in the Coast Guard*

The commander of one British boat reported two torpedo hits on the cruiser Prinz Eugen. Owing to the intensity of the barrage and heavy smoke screen the enemy was laying, it was impossible to determine the exact results of the attack. The hits that the torpedo boats had scored were the heaviest damage reported to enemy vessels. The communiqué reported that all of the MTBs returned to their base, though it was considered remarkable under the circumstances that they could even disengage themselves from the action.

### Other Channel Actions

Among the actions reported in the English Channel in which the British MTBs were involved was one only a few months ago. Patrols of light craft had located two medium-sized enemy tankers in a convoy heavily escorted by enemy small craft. The MTBs attacked — again near the Straits of Dover — scoring a torpedo hit on one of the tankers, with a possible second hit reported. Later one of these vessels was found stopped and drifting in the vicinity. Only superficial damage to the MTBs was indicated.

Among other engagements last Fall, two were reported between "patrols of light British craft" — presumably MTBs — and German torpedo boats. In one of these, two British craft fought six Nazi E-boats. Locked in combat at a range of only 200 yards for half an hour, the British sank one E-boat, despite the heavy odds against them. Two others were probably sunk in the second engagement, for they were hard hit and badly damaged.

### Bagging a Tanker with Depth Charges

One unique attack which demonstrated the ingenuity that British MTB commanders displayed in their daring raids on Nazi-held French ports was described by Lieut. Denis Germain, R.N., D.S.O., during a visit in this country to the Elco plant.

Commanding a motor torpedo boat out of Dover, he had successfully carried out a night raid during which he had run into one of the French harbors and discharged two torpedoes at ships lying there. Without tarrying to observe the results of his attack, he started back for the English coast.

Toward dawn, feeling his way through a pea-soup fog, he suddenly encountered a German tanker. The situation called for split-second thinking for Germain had used his torpedoes in the night's raid. Hesitating not an instant, he ran in under the very guns of the enemy ship, dropped a depth charge, swung around under the tanker's stern, laid another charge against the other side, and got away — fast! The ship sank.

This was the first time an MTB had gotten a surface craft with depth charges, and official cognizance of Germain's feat was taken with the award of the D.S.O.

### Evacuation of Dunkirk and Calais

Two years have elapsed since the miracle at Dunkirk, but the world has not forgotten — nor can it ever forget — the amazing accomplishments of English motor boats in the evacuation of the British Expeditionary Force.

Every conceivable type of floating craft that could be found in British ports participated in the heroic action. The role played by yachtsmen and pleasure craft has been told many times.

Four factors counted heavily in favor of the motor torpedo boats, which were conspicuous in the operations. High speed enabled them to shuttle back and forth across the Channel many times while slower craft made but a single trip. Arriving at the beach, their shallow draft permitted them to run up close enough to take men aboard directly from the water. Loading, they could take on scores of troops which craft of lesser carrying capacity could never have handled. And, finally, despite such loads, they had the maneuverability to dodge aerial attack as they ran the gantlet back to England.

In unofficial reports, nearly a dozen and a half motor torpedo boats were credited with having aided in the evacuation of approximately 100,000 troops. Loaded to the gunwales, they made their perilous passages back and forth across the Channel . . . and every boat got safely back to England!

Another story comes out of the evacuation of Calais. A small party of Royal Marines had crossed the Channel aboard a destroyer on the night of May 24-25, 1940. Fighting a covering action against overwhelming odds for forty-eight hours, they gave troops an opportunity to gather on the quays and beaches till small craft could pick them up. Among these was an MTB which took a group of survivors back to Dover.

### Chan Chak and the Hong Kong Blockade

British, Canadian and Indian troops were engaged in the last-ditch stand during which Imperial forces made against invading Japs at Hong Kong. During this siege, in which land, sea and air forces were involved, MTBs continued to operate in spite of the Japanese blockade, sinking two enemy ships.

Several days later, contrary to fantastic claims made by the enemy as to the number of torpedo boats destroyed, these same MTBs ran the Japanese blockade. Aboard was a party of British and Chinese officers led by the famous one-legged Cantonese Admiral, Chan Chak, who slipped through with a party which included the chief of the British Ministry of Information at Hong Kong, two British naval commanders, and two R.A.F. wing commanders.

### In the Waters of the World

With the spread of conflict to all the seven seas, the exploits of the motor torpedo boats are reported from almost every theater of action.

Only a few months ago, during the invasion of Java, an MTB of the Netherlands Indies forces was credited with the sinking of a Japanese flotilla leader (probably a large destroyer) in night attack in the eastern end of the Java sea.

Early in November, Kuybyshev listed the following sinkings of enemy craft by Soviet "torpedo boats" since the beginning of the war: one 6,000-ton German cruiser of the Koeln class; seven destroyers; eight transports carrying tanks and ammunition; one submarines; one 268-ton Finnish patrol vessel of the Rautu class; and one barge load of tanks. In addition they were credited with five planes and damage to other vessels. While the report does not indicate whether all of these "torpedo boats" were of the

*M. Rosenfeld*

*Elco 44 footer. Many now policing our coastlines with Coast Guard*

MTB type, it is not at all unlikely that they played, at least, a vital part.

From Borneo to the Bosporus, from Suez to Singapore, from the Baltic, from Malta, and from other Mediterranean waters, come these reports of motor torpedo boats in action.

### A Weapon of the Future

Even in the light of this impressive record of achievements, not even the staunchest advocate of the motor torpedo boat would claim it to be a weapon destined to displace ships, planes or submarines in modern warfare. All of these have their function in the machinery of total warfare.

But it is equally obvious from their exploits that PTs have shown that they fill a special niche in the program of arming nations against every contingency — that they can operate successfully under certain conditions that absolutely bar the use of any other type of vessel. Further, they have demonstrated striking power out of all proportion to their size and cost.

PTs can, and do, carry out successful attacks against tremendous odds. They have very decisively shown that they are one type of war weapon capable of tackling any kind of enemy craft — battleships, destroyers, auxiliary vessels, submarines, even planes.

Certain it is that the PT is not an outmoded weapon of the past — but a mighty weapon of the future, with which wars of the future are won.

## FROM ML TO PT

*(Continued from page 37)*

British Power Boat Company. A few years ago China joined the ranks by ordering a "suicide fleet" of Ventnor hydroplanes, with the idea of loading each with a quarter-ton of high explosives and ramming them head-on into enemy ships, at 50 m.p.h. Unfortunately, there don't seem to have been quite enough Ventnors on hand to go around.

Meantime, General Douglas MacArthur, out in the Philippines, was very much alive to the growing menace of the Japs — and to the part motor boats could play in bolstering the Island's inadequate defenses. Time was all too short, and there was little money to be had. Modern motor torpedo boats, he reasoned, can be built in something of a hurry and would provide, at minimum cost, just the sort of protection needed. A fleet of 90 — that's all it would take, he felt confident, to prevent invasion. For their extreme mobility and shallow draft would make them doubly useful: they could patrol an impressive lot of coastline, and in case of need they could concentrate quickly to do a job of "trouble-shooting."

So sure of this was the former U. S. Army Chief of Staff that he returned to the States in 1937 to sell the idea to the Navy. Some of those to whom he talked demurred, on the grounds that motor boats can't go along with the Grand Fleet. He thereupon prevailed on his old friend Admiral Leahy, then Chief of Naval Operations, to let him argue his case before a board of Navy experts.

The facts spoke for themselves; and besides, the general is a convincing talker. President Roosevelt and Secretary of the Navy Edison actively espoused the cause, got Congress to appropriate $15,000,000 in the fall of '38 for developing a suitable craft.

### Elco Tackles the Problem

Based on designs submitted in a prize contest for civilian naval architects, eight experimental PT's were built — four 59-footers and four 81-footers. But still the Navy wasn't satisfied. In January 1939, aboard a destroyer which was making a trial run out of the Kearny (N. J.) shipyards, Secretary Edison button-holed one of the guests as they were passing the Elco plant, and urged him to enter the PT field. The guest was Elco's Henry Sutphen.

*Production lines of Elco MLs during World War I*

This was almost a year before Pearl Harbor; Sutphen had no assurance of future contracts — only Edison's promise that he'd back a suitable vessel. But a month later, following up Edison's suggestion, Sutphen and the Elco designer, Irwin Chase, were on their way to England to have a look-see at the newest British MTB's. The Admiralty saw to it that they looked their fill; for these were the same two men who, nearly 25 years before, had produced the answer to German U-boat depredations.

The work Scott-Paine was doing came nearest to what Sutphen and

*Six of Elco's 39 footers delivered to the United States Army. These twin screw boats are most suitable for off-shore service*

Chase had in mind, so they put in an order for a sample 70-footer, to cost $300,000 (3 Rolls-Royce engines included). PT 9, as the boat came to be known, was delivered September 4, three days after war broke out in Europe. For ten days Navy trial board officials saw her put through her paces in New London, and Secretary Edison himself journeyed there incognito to size her up. He had five of those fifteen million dollars left, and he was anxious to put the money to good use.

### Construction Begins — Before Pearl Harbor

Confident that in certain respects they could go PT 9 several better, Elco agreed to turn out 23 more boats — turn them out at a loss, by the way. Together with PT 9 these would constitute two squadrons as a starter. Construction began in January, 1940. Because the boats lived up to expectation, and then some, additional contracts have followed in quick succession; for Secretary Knox, like President Roosevelt and former Secretary Edison, has more than a hunch that these Elco jobs will fill a highly important place in the scheme of things. (The President's interest is by no means nominal — a large and efficient mosquito fleet has been one of his pet aims ever since he served as Assistant Secretary of the Navy in the first World War.) Subsequent reports from the Philippines, based on 6 boats General MacArthur had shipped to him last October, would seem to make the verdict just about unanimous!

So once again the people at Bayonne turned to, in time of grave need, and came through with pennants flying. Operating on the principle that the best that's gone before should serve merely as a point of departure, Elco has produced a steady flow of mile-a-minute triple-screw boats, with V-12 supercharged Packard engines, which mark a considerable advance over the original PT 9.

And Elco provided its own selfstarter, mind, at a time when the nation was at peace and a heavy initial outlay was called for — with nothing to show for it on the dotted line.

### Geared Up for Mass Production

Included in that initial outlay were more than a million dollars for a brand-new Naval Division plant, which went up in 100 working days. Fenced in, flood-lighted at night, policed by uniformed guards, it houses several innovations in boat-building technique — including some the Axis would dearly like to know. Most revolutionary is the upsidedown way the hull is laid until the time arrives to right it, drop it into a waiting cradle, and move it into one of 4 assembly lines. Then too, instead of building from the hull up, step by step, prefabrication is worked for all it's worth, particularly in the superstructure. Machine tools are everywhere in evidence, and most of them are worked the clock around.

For it's a three-shift job, with 2,000-odd workers eager to hasten the day of victory. They've formed an independent union, and a special committee meets twice a month with the management to forestall any bottlenecks that might slow up production. Many a constructive idea has come out of the suggestion boxes scattered here and there. The employees are proud of their product and of its achievements, and their interest in each PT keeps up long after it has reached its destination.

Then there's that motto in the locker room: "— PTs a Week Will Make the Axis Squeak." We can't fill in the missing number, but it's nothing Hitler can laugh off. He *might* get a smile from the Walt Disney emblem that's painted on the bridge of every boat — a saucy mosquito who joyrides a torpedo. But to call Elco PTs "mosquito boats" is a misnomer. They're angry, and efficient, hornets.

A U. S. Navy Aircraft Carrier, flanked by Elco PTs, moves to sea

# ELCO-SMOKE...A CHEMICAL TRIUMPH
# THAT IS SAVING COUNTLESS LIVES!

*Elco-Smoke is a revolutionary development of Elco chemical research. A persistent white gas that hugs the water longer than former smokes, it gives more lasting protection . . . to screen our landing barges from the eyes of waiting enemy gunners . . . or to cover a PT's get-away during a bold hit-and-run attack.*

*The thick white vapor is non-burning and non-toxic to human skin and membranes. Elco-Smoke has proved to be such a great improvement over other types of smoke that the U. S. Navy has adopted it for use on many ships in addition to PTs.*

Back the Attack!

# BUY WAR BONDS

www.ingramcontent.com/pod-product-compliance
Lightning Source LLC
Chambersburg PA
CBHW081241090426
42738CB00016B/3366